Fundamentals
of Business
and Finance

Edition 1, July 2014

This learning manual covers examinations from
1 September 2014 to 31 July 2015

APPROVED WORKBOOK

Welcome to the Chartered Institute for Securities & Investment's Fundamentals of Business and Finance study material.

This learning manual has been written to prepare you for the Chartered Institute for Securities & Investment's examination.

PUBLISHED BY:
Chartered Institute for Securities & Investment
© Chartered Institute for Securities & Investment 2014
8 Eastcheap
London
EC3M 1AE
Tel: +44 20 7645 0600
Fax: +44 20 7645 0601

Written by Jonathan Haile
Reviewed by Matthew Bolton
Martin Mitchell, FCSI

This is an educational manual only and the Chartered Institute for Securities & Investment accepts no responsibility for persons undertaking trading or investments in whatever form.

While every effort has been made to ensure its accuracy, no responsibility for loss occasioned to any person acting or refraining from action as a result of any material in this publication can be accepted by the publisher or authors.

A Learning Map, which contains the full syllabus, appears at the end of this workbook. The syllabus can also be viewed on the Institute's website at cisi.org and is also available by contacting Customer Support on +44 20 7645 0777. Please note that the exam is based on the syllabus.

Candidates are reminded to check the Candidate Update area of the Institute's website (cisi.org/candidateupdate) on a regular basis for updates that could affect their exam as a result of industry change.

The questions contained in this workbook are designed as an aid to revision of different areas of the syllabus and to help you consolidate your learning chapter by chapter. They should not be seen as a 'mock' exam and are not necessarily indicative of the level of the questions in the corresponding exam.

Studybook version: 1.1 (July 2014)

Learning with the CISI

You are now studying for an exam that will introduce you to the Fundamentals of Business and Finance, showing how the industry works, especially markets. This workbook and the elearning product is designed to provide you with interesting information and to enable you to know more about and understand this very important industry.

You may not have heard of the CISI, but we have around 40,000 members, who are already in relevant work. We hope that this exam will help you to build awareness of career opportunities and personal financial knowledge. Whether you are in work, or education, you will find this useful.

When you register for the exam, you will be able to access a wide range of resources on our website (cisi.org) which will not only help with your studies, but help to broaden awareness of all aspects of the investment and banking world.

We hope that this thorough grounding in the essentials will encourage you to consider financial services as a career option.

This workbook and elearning product are updated annually, so please check to ensure you have the correct version for your exam. As well as using industry specialists to update and review the material, we also use students and tutors to ensure that the material is relevant to your needs and level of experience.

We really hope that you enjoy your studies with the CISI and that you find the learning experience a stimulating one.

With best wishes for your studies.

Ruth Martin, Managing Director

Buying and Selling 1

The Value of Money Now and in the Future 17

Risk and Reward 31

Protection from Risks 45

Competing for our Money 55

The Role of Governments in an Economy 65

The Role of the Private Sector in an Economy 75

The Function of Markets 85

Planning for the Future 97

The Ethics of Business 107

Glossary and Abbreviations 115

Multiple Choice Questions 123

Syllabus Learning Map 133

It is estimated that this workbook will require approximately 30 hours of study time.

Buying and Selling

1. Introduction   3

2. Buying and Selling   4

3. Saving and Borrowing   7

4. Foreign Exchange and Exchange Rates   10

5. The Fundamentals of Trading   12

6. Trading of Shares and other Securities   13

This syllabus area will provide approximately 4 of the 30 examination questions

Buying and Selling

1. Introduction

The objective of this workbook is to give readers a knowledge of **business** and **finance** as it works today, in our computerised global village, connected by the worldwide web. Though the tools have changed, the basic disciplines are little altered since one of our cavemen ancestors sold the latest flint stone spear to a hunter, for a share of the next ten deer he killed, thus initiating the first credit transaction.

Mankind's first transactions were in the form of **barter,** the exchange of goods or services in payment. However, barter has severe disadvantages. It can be difficult to value. For instance, how large will the haunch of venison be? What happens if it arrives when the purchaser already has one in the larder? There is no guarantee that what is offered will be attractive to the other party. What was required was a store of value that was agreed, was transportable and always attractive, so that

it could be used to purchase other goods when required. Metal became the preferred medium of exchange when our ancestors discovered how to extract it and turn it into useful items. It ticked all the boxes with its portability being improved as the attractiveness of precious metals increased and it was possible to have a store of value in a small volume. It was easier to have silver and gold in your pocket rather than a chunk of bronze or iron in the back of a wagon!

Coins were first produced around 700BC in Asia Minor, with paper money being invented in China around 1100AD. The use of a recognised store of value immensely increased trading both within nations and internationally. Goods could be priced in a generally accepted denomination and sellers knew what they were getting in exchange for their goods. The design stamped on the coin not only indicated its value, but also guaranteed its genuineness, with the authority and might of the state standing behind it. That authority and might depended on the power and repute of the issuing state, but traders soon came to recognise and make allowance for that. The stater of Persia, the drachma of Macedonia and the denarius of Rome were the ancient world's equivalents of the British pound and the US dollar in international trade.

Even a thousand years before the Christian Era, there was International trade. Silk and spices came from the Far East, while Cornwall, which provided the world's tin, a vital ingredient of bronze of which the world's utensils and weapons were made, was the equivalent of a modern oil state like Abu Dhabi. With trade came banking and international finance.

This workbook is designed to introduce you to the fundamentals of business and finance. A Roman trader brought forward 2,000 years might find our computers bewildering but he would immediately recognise the underlying business.

2. Buying and Selling

Learning Objective 1

Candidates must know that price is established by the interaction of buyers and sellers. In all markets – including those for financial products – traders try to profit from the difference between the buying price and the selling price

2.1 Specialisation and Trade

Learning Objective 1.1

How specialisation has led to a need for a system of trade; how a trading system based on barter gave way to a system based on money

No unit of living, whether a house, a town, a city or a country, can be self-sufficient unless it is prepared to do without the benefits of those goods that it cannot produce itself. Specialisation arrived early in mankind's history, particularly with the discovery of metals. Obviously, metal can only be mined where there is sufficient in the ground to make it worthwhile. Given the inefficiency of early transport systems, it made sense to smelt metal where it was mined, rather than transporting the ore. It also made sense

for miners to exchange their product for all their other necessities and, indeed, luxuries, rather than waste their time, producing their own food and clothing. Specialisation arose for a whole range of reasons. The local topography can favour a form of production that other areas do not. For instance, sheep flourished on the hills of Spain and England, which were responsible for clothing much of Europe in the middle ages and these countries grew rich on the production of wool. In England, the Lord Chancellor still sits upon the Woolsack in the House of Lords, while in Spain, the premier order of knighthood is the Order of the Golden Fleece, reflecting, in their different ways, the importance of wool in their economies.

Specialisation can also occur where a concentration on an industry creates an area of expertise that feeds on itself. For instance, the great Italian cities of Genoa and Venice were responsible for much of the trade in luxuries from the Far East that mediaeval and Renaissance Europe wished to purchase. With trade came banking and there is still a Lombard Street in the City of London where the English branches of the great Northern Italian banking houses could be found. Many of these went bankrupt when the King of England refused to pay his debts but the name remains and the street is still full of banks.

2.2 Price

Learning Objective 1.1.1

How money has made price the basis of trade and how markets enable buyers and sellers to come together

The invention of money and its adoption as a means of exchange, largely ending the use of barter, meant that goods and services could be priced in a generally accepted and easily recognisable format. No longer was every transaction a matter for negotiation over exchanges for goods which were difficult to value. For instance, Mr Baker would no longer have to accept one of Mr Hatter's hats for his loaves of bread and hope that he could exchange it for a barrel of Mr Brewer's beer. The coin of the realm – money – stood in the middle of each transaction as a form of **intermediation**.

It also meant that the price of goods and services could be compared easily because they were all priced using the same mechanism. It was still necessary to compare the different qualities or expertises on offer but this was always against money.

2.3 Intermediation and Markets

Money has already been described as a form of intermediation – something that stands in the middle of a transaction. Traders and retailers can also be described as intermediaries. They do not produce the goods or services that they offer but stand in the middle as a convenience between producers and purchasers.

You only have to look at any town centre to realise that intermediaries like to gather together. It is obviously convenient for purchasers if the butcher, the baker and the candlestick maker are all next to each other. It makes shopping so much easier. Supermarkets and shopping malls take the concept of the high street to the next level.

Where specialist traders gather together, you have a market. In London, the meat traders gathered at Smithfield, the fishmongers at Billingsgate and the fruit and flower sellers at Covent Garden. Just like the traders of physical goods, so the traders in financial products gathered together, largely in the City of London. You can find the traders in stocks and shares at the Stock Exchange, insurance brokers at Lloyd's of London and bankers' headquarters near the Bank of England. Now that financial products are merely blips on the computer and trading takes place over the internet, many of the physical markets no longer exist but the markets themselves still do, though now on the web.

2.4 The Pricing Mechanism and Supply and Demand

Learning Objective 1.1.2

How wants are unlimited and resources are scarce; how markets establish a balance between those wants and the supply of resources to satisfy them

Learning Objective 1.1.3

How price will adjust to the level at which demand is willing to buy and supply is willing to sell; how price signals that a good or service is in short or plentiful supply

The pricing of goods is a balance between the cost of production and what purchasers are prepared to pay for them. It is also a balance between supply and demand. These balances are very fluid as the various factors influence each other. For instance, if supply and demand are evenly balanced, the price can be fixed at a level at which the two are equal. However, if the cost of production increases, producers will want to increase the price. At the higher price, more producers may find it profitable to make the goods, while fewer purchasers may find it worthwhile to buy them. The result is that supply and demand are no longer in balance and producers can no longer sell all the goods that they produce. Some producers will stop production and others will cut their price with the result that the balance moves the other way and more purchasers appear for fewer goods. So the balance changes again.

The history of the price of oil over the last half century gives a good example of how supply and demand have changed with the changing of the price and how the altered price has, in turn, changed supply and demand. Oil is a central requirement in modern economies, responsible for transport, heating, power and manufacture, as a core constituent of plastics. The failure of a country to obtain sufficient oil would cripple its economy.

You can see in Figure 1, a chart showing the oil prices since 1973. There were two big jumps in price in 1973 and 1979 when the Organization of Petroleum Exporting Countries

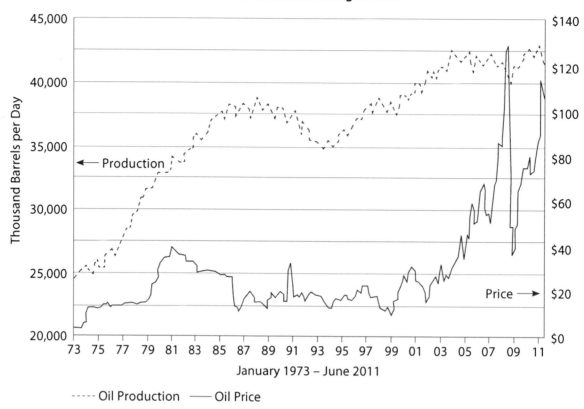

Crude Oil Production (Mbbl/d)
Non-OPEC Countries Average/Totals

----- Oil Production   —— Oil Price

Source: WTRG Economics (2011)

Figure 1

(OPEC), representing the middle eastern and South American producers, raised the price unilaterally in reaction to the Israeli wars. The result of the price rise was to make extracting oil from environmentally hostile places, such as Alaska and the North Sea, much more economically viable. There was a sharp drop in the price of oil as these new sources came on stream and the price of oil remained fairly stable, with new production balancing out increased demand until the boom in demand in the early years of the new millennium coincided with reduced production from the areas developed in the mid 1980s. The financial crash brought about a crash in the oil price which recovered as the Far East took up much of the slack. The second decade of this century has seen the effect of fracking in the US. Fracking is the extraction of natural gas and oil from shale and through the injection of water and chemicals. Fracking has seen the US move from being a major importer of oil to exporting both oil and gas. If fracking continues to expand in Europe, it is likely that we will see the price of oil remain steady or even continue to fall.

2.5   Pricing and Technology

Fracking is a good example of another major influence on prices–new technology and new production methods. These have always changed supply and demand and the last half century has seen an immense acceleration in progress and it is likely that this will continue. The improvement in modern communication has meant that new technology that would once have taken centuries to cross the world now does so in a flash.

2.6 Seasonality and Supply and Demand

The most obvious example of prices changing over the year is, for most people, the price of holidays. The price of a seaside holiday will be highest in July and August, both because that is when the weather is best and also because that is when children are out of school. The actual cost to the provider is little different between a miserable week in February and a lovely sunny week in July but the demand will have increased out of all comparison and so will the price. Most holiday providers break even at best in the low season and make all their profit in the high season.

3. Saving and Borrowing

Learning Objective 1.2

How a trading system based on money leads to the build-up of surpluses (more money than people need for their day-to-day expenses) and deficits (not enough money for day-to-day expenses)

Money is the grease that oils the wheels of trade. It is also the constant against which goods and services are measured. However, it is also a commodity in its own right, with a value and the ability to be profitable like any other commodity. Money is not evenly spread across the population. It grows in piles, with some people having more than they need, while others have less than they require. It could be said that the minimum people require is a sufficiency to cover their daily needs. However, 'daily needs' can expand whenever the money available to cover them has grown, so that the needs of a billionaire will usually be much greater than those of someone who has just started work in a lowly position. Moreover, what is classed as frugal behaviour by the former would be rank extravagance in the latter.

Experience will have taught you that, at any point in time, some people hold money in the form of credit balances at the bank and others will owe money in the form of debit balances. Moreover, over a period of time, which may be

a lifetime, a year, a month, the same individual can move from being in credit to being in debit and back again. Indeed, an individual may have both credit and debit balances at the same time, such as a credit balance on the current account and a hefty debit in the form of a mortgage. The same situation occurs with companies and, indeed, governments, though generally on a larger scale than with individuals. Short-term credits for individuals will take the form of credit balances on the current account, or indeed, cash in the pocket, while short-term debits can be met by an overdraft facility, which is expected to be paid off when the salary check hits the account, or with credit cards.

3.1 Depositors

Learning Objective 1.2.1

How savers (who have surplus money) seek to earn a return on their spare cash by charging interest

Those who have credit balances with an institution such as a bank are generally called **depositors.** They are also legally **creditors** since the institution owes them the money that has been deposited, even if the institution considers that it is doing the depositor a service by looking after the money. If the money is deposited for a longer term, it can be regarded as saving and the saver will look for a premium for depositing the funds for a longer term, such as **interest**. The 'interest' on a current account is often paid in the form of **free banking**, with the institution not paying interest and the depositor not paying for the banking service.

3.2 Borrowers

Learning Objective 1.2.2

How borrowers (who are short of money) have to pay interest to those who are willing to lend it to them

Those who do not have the cash available to meet their needs have to borrow and become debtors of the lender. The debt maybe a few pounds to cover expenditure to the end of the month before payday, a debit on the credit card to pay for a bargain in the sales to be paid off over the next few months or a major sum to pay for a house to be paid off over a lifetime. Once again, such money commands a **price** and that price is the interest paid by the borrower.

3.3   Intermediaries

It is possible for borrowers to go to friends or family for the money they require (the Bank of Mum and Dad!), but there are many reasons why this may not be possible. Apart from the fact that they may not have the funds available, there is also embarrassment in asking and it may cause difficulties in the relationship if it is not possible for the borrower to repay when the lender wants the money back. As a result, most depositors and borrowers will go to an institution such as a bank or building society. Such institutions will stand in between depositors and borrowers – an intermediary.

Intermediaries offer major benefits to both the depositor and the borrower, apart from the security that their size and creditworthiness provide. That security may be increased by either an explicit or implied government guarantee. The size of the institution's business allows it to lend short-term deposits to long-term borrowers in the expectation that they will always be able to meet the demands of the depositors requiring money back, because fresh deposits are always being made. They are also able to spread the cost of risk across all borrowers in the expectation that only a proportion of borrowers will fail to pay them back and their experience over many years allows them to judge what that proportion is likely to be.

3.4   Lending Spread

Learning Objective 1.2.3

How banks and building societies work as intermediaries between savers and borrowers and charge a higher rate for lending to borrowers than they pay out to the savers

Lenders, such as banks and building societies, make their profit from the difference between what it costs them on deposits and what they charge on loans. Although, with regard to costs, it is easiest just to look at the interest paid on deposits, it must be remembered that there are a number of other costs that must be factored in, such as administration, losses on loans that have not been repaid and reserve costs etc.

Equally, on loans the banks will charge not only interest, but also setup charges, early repayment charges and administration charges, where these are appropriate. Even deposits that appear to be free to the banks, such as credit balances on current accounts, actually incur heavy administrative costs for running branch, computer and automated teller machine (ATM) networks. The calculation on appropriate interest rates for both deposits and loans is therefore highly complex even where it would be expected that the sole driver is what the market dictates. It is the calculation on profitability that dictates where individual banks direct their marketing effort.

Money is **fungible.** In other words, there is no difference between one pound and another. Just because the £20 note you have deposited is immediately handed out as a withdrawal to another customer does not mean that it is your money that has been given out. As mentioned above, banks are therefore able to lend money long-term, such as on mortgages, that they may have borrowed very short-term, such as credit account balances which are repayable on demand. Banks rely on confidence in their long-term future, since no bank in the world could repay all, or even a very small proportion of its depositors, if they simultaneously asked for their money back. Northern Rock and Bradford & Bingley discovered this in the 2007 financial crash, when both failed and their depositors had to be rescued by the government.

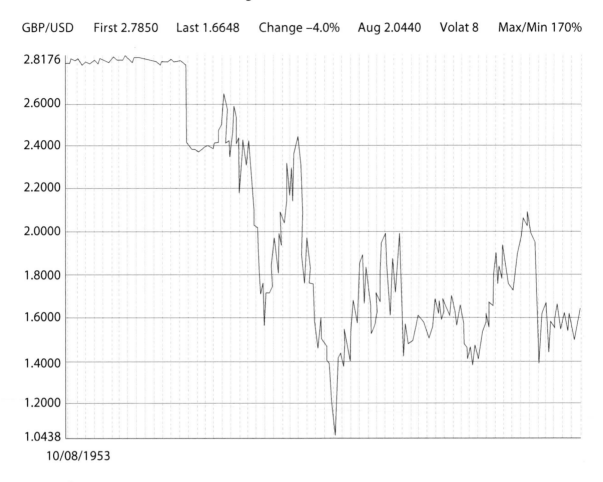

£GB Rate Against the US$
August 1953 to March 2014

GBP/USD   First 2.7850   Last 1.6648   Change –4.0%   Aug 2.0440   Volat 8   Max/Min 170%

Source: fxtop.com (2013)

Figure 2

4. Foreign Exchange and Exchange Rates

Learning Objective 1.3

How the system of foreign exchange markets allows one currency to be exchanged for another to facilitate international trade, either for immediate or future delivery

Learning Objective 1.3.2

How foreign exchange transactions are conducted; how a foreign exchange dealer makes a profit by selling a currency at a higher price and buying the currency back at a lower price

The most usual foreign exchange transaction that most people in this country will experience is the purchase of foreign currency to spend on their holiday overseas. Although this represents only an incredibly small proportion of the currency trades undertaken in the UK, the basics of the transaction reflect the basics of all currency transactions. The bank will sell currency to you at one price and offer to repurchase the currency at another price that is considerably lower. For instance, let us assume that you purchase US dollars for your holiday and return with exactly the same number of dollars with which you started. The sums could therefore look like this:

£100 @ US$1.6/£1   =   US$160

$160 @ US$1.7/£1   =   £94.12

As you can see, your currency transaction has cost you nearly 6% of your initial sum. The spread between your purchase and sale price reflects not only the bank's profit but also the costs of administering the transaction and transporting and guarding the physical currency.

As soon as goods or services are imported or exported, it is likely that a currency transaction will be incurred. For instance, a manufacturer in the UK will require sterling to pay his wages bill etc, while the retailer to whom he sells in the US wants to pay in US dollars which is what he will receive in his shops. Once again, an intermediary in the shape of a currency trader, usually one of the international banks, will step in and carry out the currency transaction to facilitate the export of goods from the UK and the import of the same goods to the US. Either the currency trader will have another client with the opposite requirement or he will go to another trader to carry out the other side of those transactions. He will expect to do the transaction at a profit, by buying at a lower price than the one at which he sells.

It is obvious that the wider the spread at which the currency trader can deal, the better the profit. If all his transactions were with small or medium-sized importers and exporters, the trader's ability to widen the spread would be improved. As soon as the trader has to transact with another major bank, his ability to obtain a profitable spread will be severely restricted. We therefore meet the other factor in profitable currency trading, that is the magic of big numbers.

The numbers involved in currency trading are very large indeed. The <u>daily</u> world turnover in foreign currencies is worth around US$5 trillion and around 40% of this is transacted in London, the largest market in the world. Even if the average profit on a transaction is a tiny fraction of 1%, the contribution of currency trading to the bank's profits can be very significant.

4.1 Exchange Rate Movement

Learning Objective 1.3.1
How most currencies in the world move up and down in relation to other currencies

Learning Objective 1.3.3
How strong demand for a currency will push up its price relative to other currencies and weaker demand will pull its price down

Figure 2 above shows the GB£ rate against the US$ from August 1953 to March 2014. From the point of view of British traders, importers and exporters, this is probably the most important rate to watch, not only because of the importance of the US as a market, but also because so much of the world's trade, particularly oil and other commodities, is priced in dollars.

Exchange rates used to be fixed. Any movement was generally made by the government of the day and moved from one fixed price to another. You can see the last time a government move of this type was made by the British Government in 1967 when the value of the pound moved from $2.8 to $2.4. Since 15 August 1971, exchange rates have moved in compliance with the market and flows of money around the world. These flows are dictated by a number of influences.

1. **Trade.** A successful exporting nation, of which Germany is the prime example in Europe, has more currency coming into the country in payment for exports, than it is paying out for imports. The result, in pre-European Union (EU) days, was that the German mark consistently strengthened against other currencies, particularly against the British pound. Even now that Germany is part of the EU, the success of its economy has a major influence on the performance of the euro. Germany's success is largely based on the performance of its manufacturing sector with the names of Volkswagen, BMW and Siemens, for instance, known all round the world. However, it must be remembered that not all exports are physical. Britain's strength over the last quarter-century has been in service export and particularly in financial services, based in the City of London.

The success of London's foreign exchange market was mentioned at the start of section 3, but the metals exchange, stock exchange and insurance (Lloyds of London), are also leaders in their industries. Other notable contributors to the balance of payments have been music (from the Beatles onwards), fashion and tourism. The benefits from these are generally classed as **invisibles** and have so far always been positive for the UK.

2. **Investment.** Countries, companies and wealthy individuals all need to deposit their surplus funds somewhere safe and profitable and also capable of absorbing their funds and being able to pay them out again should the need arise. Political stability and being a large economy are major requirements. It is therefore no surprise that the US is the prime target for investors, boosted by the fact that much of the world's trade in commodities is priced in US dollars. Britain, the EU and Switzerland have also been targets, while more recently, China and other emerging nations have also joined the list. Much of this investment is in the form of government loans, particularly to the US and the UK.

3. **Economic and social weakness.** Frequently, economic and social weakness go together, but not always. It may be that a part of the economy is very strong, particularly if there are commodities involved, but the social weakness means that the bulk of the economy does not benefit, since the profits are siphoned out illegally. However, if a country is weak and badly governed, investment is not made, capital is sent abroad and the brightest and most go-ahead individuals do their utmost to leave the country. This is generally reflected in a weak currency.

4. **peculation.** This is regularly the reason given by politicians seeking to divert attention from their own failures. However, speculators only like to gamble on what looks like a certainty, particularly if a currency is overvalued because of government action. In other words, speculators will reinforce the direction of a currency's movement, determined by one or more of the three reasons above. They do not change the entire direction of a currency by their actions.

5. **Market sentiment.** The market can get it wrong, though this is more usually temporary than a permanent phenomenon. Markets are more likely to continue in the same direction as previously, without recognising that the fundamentals have changed. The result is often a more rapid correction, or crash, than would have happened had the error not occurred. Markets are driven by greed and fear and these two can cause traders to lose sight of reason.

The result of these underlying reasons is that currencies move against each other. If money flows into a country, the currency will improve and, conversely, if it flows out, the currency rate will fall. These movements are generally not smooth and a glance at Figure 2 above shows that even where there is a definite trend, there are frequent movements against the trend.

4.2 Forward Foreign Exchange Rates

If you go into the bank to purchase currency, the bank will use the rate of the day, generally known as the spot rate, to calculate the amount of currency to give you in exchange for your British pounds. However, importers and exporters usually wish to fix a rate for a transaction that will take place sometime in the future.

For instance, a manufacturer may close a deal to export a product to the US six months from the day of the agreement. As part of the deal, the purchaser requests three months' credit after delivery to allow him to sell the product to his customer and get the cash in. The exporter knows that he will receive US dollars in nine months' time but wishes to fix the rate now, so will undertake a forward currency deal with his bank to exchange dollars for sterling at that time. The rate that the bank quotes will reflect the time lag and so will be different from the spot rate. However, the exporter knows how many pounds will be credited to his account and in the meantime, has insured himself against currency movements that could alter the profitability of the original transaction. He has the certainty he requires to plan his future production.

The two basic foreign exchange transactions are spot (immediate settlement) and forward (settlement at an agreed time in the future). All other types of foreign exchange transactions, such as options or swaps, are variations on the theme of achieving a foreign exchange transaction either now or at some future time.

5.   The Fundamentals of Trading

Learning Objective 1.4

How the desire for profit will encourage buyers to try to pay as low a price as possible and sellers to charge as high a price as possible

Learning Objective 1.4.1

In a normal market, traders will always seek to sell a product at a price which is higher than the price they paid to acquire that product in the first place

In any type of business, the objective is to buy as cheaply as possible and to sell at as high a price as possible. If there is a monopoly, the seller will try to set the highest price possible, until buyers decide that it is not worth buying the goods. If there are a number of sellers, the price will settle where no competitor is prepared to undercut, since the increase in sales will not increase the profitability of the transactions. However, there are a number of requirements for traders which are not necessary for a retailer.

1   **A market.** You cannot trade if you have nowhere to do your trading. In this context, a market is a collection of traders. Though, originally, a market was regarded as a place, the important fact was the connectivity between traders that close proximity allowed. Modern communications allow the same degree of connectivity, even if traders are half a world apart.

2   **An adequate volume of trades.** Traders thrive on volume of trades. The magic of big numbers was explained at the start of Section 3 when talking about foreign exchange, but the same applies to any market. The larger the volume, the tighter the margins can be and still be profitable. This, in turn, encourages further turnover.

3   **Hedging** is the ability to insure against losses if the market moves against the trader. This allows a trader to buy, or sell, a larger amount than he would like to keep, in the knowledge that he can offload a proportion of the trade to another trader. All traders play pass the parcel, whether they be a major international bank, trading in billions every day, or a bookie at the local race course with a turnover measured in hundreds. The ability to do so is a vital part of a market's workings that the general public does not see.

5.1   Profits from Trading

Learning Objective 1.4.2

Trading is usually profitable if the gap (or spread) between the buying price and selling price is wide enough

If one can buy an asset and then sell the same asset at a higher price then an element of profit will result. The wider the difference between the two prices, the greater will be the profit.

The word "spread" refers to the difference between the highest buying price and the lowest selling price active for a specific product or security available in the market at a particular moment in time. This is known as the bid/ask spread or the bid/offer spread, where "bid" refers to the buying price. If the difference is small, spreads are said to be narrow. If far apart, the spread is described as being wide. Narrow spreads indicate good liquidity in the market.

In securities markets, the spread narrows as the difference between the bid price and ask price for a security is reduced. Market makers, a group of specialist traders active on most markets with a remit to support market liquidity, will narrow the spread as trading in a particular security becomes more active and competition increases.

Profits and losses derived from the buying and selling of any asset on any market depend on the price levels achieved and market timing. The old adage is "buy low and sell high". This obviously makes sense at first sight but the outturn cannot be guaranteed. It is an objective rather than a right. Do not assume that profit is made on every trade; that is not how things work. Some sellers may be forced to sell whatever the price; the same might be true of some buyers. Hence the profit or loss generated will vary. There are always two parties to any trade – the buyer and the seller. The price of any executed (agreed) transaction has to involve these two parties, by definition. They are each entering the market for a variety of reasons. They will both not automatically make a profit. One trader's profit is another's loss in simple terms. This is because market prices move all the time and do so extremely rapidly. Markets react to supply and demand, which in turn is driven by information and news.

Buying low and selling high are obviously keynotes for success in trading but the spread is a reflection of the state at the present moment in the market and can change in an instant. It can also widen and narrow as well as the overall market level moving higher or lower. Hence, if a trader bought an asset now by meeting the asking selling price (by definition), when he came to sell back the asset to the market meeting the then buyer's price, both the market level and the spread may have changed. This would hold true whatever time had elapsed since the asset was first bought.

5.2   Narrow and Wide Spreads

Learning Objective 1.4.3

The size of the spread is the trader's profit margin. The narrower the spread, the less profit the trader is likely to make; the wider the spread, the more profit

The spread would be the profit if a trader were able to buy and sell the same number of contracts or securities simultaneously in the market by selling at the ask price and buying at the bid price. As indicated, market timing is of crucial importance. A good example is provided by the market makers – the specialist traders who support the liquidity in the market. They do this by quoting to all participants in the market continuous two-way prices (bids and offers), which they modify constantly in a competitive environment against other market makers. Assuming a market maker was able to buy and sell to other market participants at the same moment the same number of identical securities, the market maker's profit on those two particular trades would be the size of the spread. The wider the spread the greater would be the profit.

Market timing however presents a major impediment to the market maker's ability to achieve this.

6.   Trading of Shares and Other Securities

Learning Objective 1.5

Companies sell shares to members of the public in return for investment capital

A market for trading shares and securities is generally known as a stock exchange or a bourse. Shares represent a part holding in the ownership of a company. Each share may only represent a tiny part of the company (a major company like Shell has tens of billions of shares) but nevertheless each one shares (hence the name) in the profits and income of the company. Equally importantly, their share of the losses of a company is limited to the amount of money paid for the share. If a company becomes bankrupt, creditors cannot force the shareholders to pay for the losses. Shareholders can lose 100% of their investment but no more. The invention of limited liability has been a major driver of the growth of western economies over the last four centuries. If you look at the names of companies in the UK, you will see that they are described as either Limited (Ltd) or public limited company (plc).

6.1 Primary Market

The primary market is where the existing shareholders (who maybe the founders of the company) wish to sell in order to realise their investment in the business or the company itself needs to raise money for investment to expand or to cover losses made. Google and Facebook are examples of the first two while Lloyds Bank and Royal Bank of Scotland (RBS) are sad examples of the latter. The term **primary market** ultimately refers to the marketing of new shares in a company to investors for the first time.

6.2 Secondary Market

Learning Objective 1.5.1

Shares can be bought and sold on stock exchanges. The selling price will nearly always be higher than the buying price

---

Those selling on the primary market will find it difficult to interest investors if the buyers are not assured of being able to sell the shares in due course. As a result, a secondary market sprang up, starting in a coffee shop in the City of London and expanding to the global phenomenon of stock exchanges. Like all markets, there are intermediaries involved.

Stockbrokers interact with members of the public who wish to buy and sell shares and who pass their orders to the stockbrokers. Stockbrokers in turn arrange the orders with other intermediaries often referred to as market makers.

As with all markets, market makers will offer two prices: a lower price at which they will buy from the public and a higher price at which they will sell to investors. Prices will move depending on the general trend of orders. If there are more buyers than sellers, the price will rise, and if there are more sellers than buyers the price will fall. By and large, prices will keep in line since the other market makers will rapidly take advantage of any of their colleagues falling out of line. There will be a smaller margin in the prices quoted for high-volume shares, such as those in FTSE 100 companies, than in low-

volume shares since in the former, the market makers can rely on the magic of big numbers for their profit.

Of all the major markets in the UK, the stock market is the one that will impinge on most people's lives since nearly everyone invests in shares, whether directly or indirectly through investment funds, pensions and life insurance.

📃 Chapter Questions

Based on what you have learned in Chapter One, try to answer the following questions.

Think of an answer for each question and refer to the appropriate section for confirmation.

1. What are the benefits of using money rather than barter?

    Answer reference: Section 1

    ....

    ....

2. What is the role of intermediaries in a trade?

    Answer reference: Section 2.3

    ....

    ....

3. What can happen to supply and demand if the price of goods is raised?

    Answer reference: Section 2.4

    ....

    ....

4. What is the role of intermediaries in banking and finance?

    Answer reference: Section 3.3

    ....

    ....

5. What is the purpose of forward exchange?

    Answer reference: Section 4.2

    ....

    ....

Fundamentals of Business and Finance

2

The Value of Money Now and in the Future

1. Buy Now or Pay Later   19

2. Inflation and Deflation   20

3. Interest   23

4. Types and Costs of Borrowing   26

This syllabus area will provide approximately 4 of the 30 examination questions

The Value of Money Now and In the Future

Learning Objective 2

Money in our pocket today is valued more highly than the promise of the same amount of money in the future. This is due to time preference and the desire to avoid erosion of buying power by inflation

As discussed in Chapter 1, money fulfils a number of roles. It is a measure of value; it is a store of value; it is an intermediate in transactions; it is a commodity. However, one thing it is not is a **constant**. The value of money changes over time and it has more value to its owners depending on when they hold it. By and large, money now is worth more than money in the future, though this is not always the case. For instance, pension saving is one example where it is judged better to defer the enjoyment of money. This chapter explains why this is so and how the differences arise.

1. Buy Now or Pay Later

Learning Objective 2.1

Goods or services available now are preferred to otherwise identical goods available in the future

If it were not for credit, it would always be necessary to save up until you had sufficient cash to buy whatever you wanted. The ability to borrow means that, so long as your credit is good enough, it is possible to decide whether to purchase an object now or wait until you can do it without borrowing. In making the decision, it is necessary to decide whether the value of possessing the asset now is worth the extra cost that credit will entail. Do the benefits outweigh the disadvantages? The benefit of a purchase may only be the joy of possession of, say, a pair of shoes, in which case the benefit is easy to calculate. However, other purchases provide benefits as well as costs. A house, for instance, provides shelter and somewhere to live. Given the rise in house prices it may also be a profitable investment. A failure to buy a house early on in your career may make it impossible to buy one later as the rise in the price may outstrip the growth in your income.

1.1   Time Preference

Learning Objective 2.1.1

People are prepared to pay more to have the use of a good or service immediately, rather than wait to save up for it – hence the popularity of credit cards

Buying now with credit may be beneficial in the longer term, in spite of the extra costs, but the costs and benefits should be part of the calculation before the purchase. As a rough rule of thumb, any debt incurred in the purchase of an asset should be paid off within the lifetime of the asset. The debt on a pair of shoes should be paid off within weeks; on a holiday, before the holiday is taken; on a house, the debt can take a lifetime to pay off and still be beneficial.

1.2   Opportunity Cost

Learning Objective 2.1.2

Money available now can be invested to generate income; if the money is tied up elsewhere for a long time, that missed opportunity is a cost

The opportunity cost of a purchase can be defined as the loss of an opportunity to do something else with the money. If the amount of money is limited, the purchase of, say, a car could be at the expense of decorating the house or of investing in a pension, or paying off existing debt. The opportunity cost should always be considered before making a significant purchase.

2.   Inflation and Deflation

2.1   Inflation

Learning Objective 2.2.1

A general increase in the level of prices

Inflation can be defined as a general increase in the prices of goods without any proportionate increase in the quality of goods. If there is more money available to purchase goods, but the quantity of goods remains the same, it follows that the price of goods will rise. This can become a vicious circle as, to compensate for the rising prices, workers force management to increase their wages. Management, therefore, has to increase the price of the goods they make to compensate for the higher wages. At this point, workers request another pay rise. Figure 3 shows how inflation has moved in the UK since the end of the First World War.

The highest rates of inflation were suffered during the two World Wars and during the 1970s. During the former, both labour that was not in the Armed Forces and goods were scarce and as a result, the price of both rose sharply. In the 1970s government and management lost control of wages at a time that unions enjoyed their greatest power.

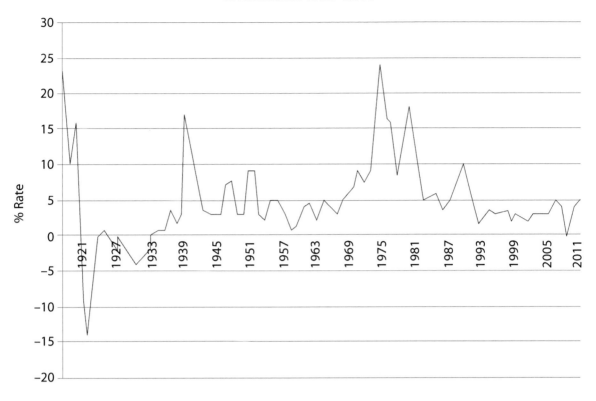

UK Inflation 1921-2011

Source: ONS
Figure 3

2.2 The Effect of Inflation

Learning Objective 2.2

What inflation is and how it erodes the value of financial assets

Learning Objective 2.2.2

How inflation erodes the buying power of money over time

Not all the effects of inflation will be considered perverse by those who live through it. Assets, and particularly property, will rise in price. Debt, on the other hand, will fall in value as generally the interest paid will remain the same in money terms, but fall in buying power. Those who bought houses at the beginning of the 1970s saw the value of their property rise sharply while the mortgage remained the same but, given the effects of inflation on their salary, became a much smaller multiple of their salary.

Those on fixed incomes, largely those who lived off their savings, particularly the retired, suffered badly while those who enjoyed indexed salaries and pensions or who were able to negotiate rises in income ahead of the rises in prices became better off. The effect of runaway inflation on the economy as a whole is generally woeful. The price of goods rises exponentially and as a result, the goods become less attractive to those who wish to buy exports. Even a fall in the exchange rate will not compensate for the inflationary rise in the price of exports, while it will make imports more expensive and contribute to the rate of inflation. One of the typical cartoon pictures of the hyperinflation suffered by Germany between the World Wars was of individuals having to use a wheelbarrow to cart all the money needed to buy a loaf of bread to the shops.

2.3 Deflation

This is when prices decrease rather than increase, the exact opposite of inflation. While, at first glance, it may seem that falling prices are beneficial to shoppers, this is only so when the price falls because of improvements in technology, economies of scale and productivity. When prices fall because nobody will buy, because they have insufficient funds and sellers have to reduce prices to tempt buyers in, the only answer they have is to lay staff off. So there are more people with no money and the vicious circle continues. Property prices fall, exposing borrowers to negative equity and increasing the risk for banks. Fortunately, in the UK, there has not been deflation since the 1920s. It is easier for governments to resort to the printing presses to create more money, thus stoking inflation, than create the scenario that produces deflation. However, in countries such as Greece, which is tied to the euro, the creation of more money has been forbidden and the remedies used by the UK, which followed quantitative easing, not allowed. The resulting deflation has created massive unemployment, particularly amongst the young, of whom around 50% are unemployed.

2.4 Using Indices to Measure Inflation

Learning Objective 2.2.3

How to construct a basic binary index

Governments, employers, economists and many others need to be able to measure the change in the cost of living. This is done by creating indices, which measure how prices change generally. A basket of goods is selected that mirrors the expenditure of households over a period of time. These are then weighted to reflect the impact on the family budget. For instance, a loaf of bread and a television are both likely to be on a shopping list at some time, but while the loaf, which is relatively cheap, may be bought three times a week, the expensive television will only be bought once in, say, three years.

2.5 Consumer Price Index (CPI)

Learning Objective 2.2.4

How governments use CPI to measure the impact of inflation on their citizens

It is possible to construct different indices to reflect different lifestyles. The shopping basket of a family with young children will be very different from that of a pensioner. The government also ensures, in official indices, that the tools they use for managing the economy, such as interest rates, are left out. The two indices most used are the Retail Prices Index (RPI) and the Consumer Price Index (CPI) with the latter being used most for adjusting benefits.

The CPI contains 700 items and prices are collected from around 120,000 different retailing outlets on a monthly basis and include both goods and services. The CPI is also used as the measure by which the Bank of England controls interest rates. The Bank of England is tasked by the Government with maintaining the annual inflation rate, as measured by the CPI, at 2%. The Governor of the Bank of England has to write a letter to the Chancellor of the Exchequer explaining the reason when the target has been missed.

3.   Interest

Learning Objective 2.3

Interest is the price of money. It can be described as the 'rent' that owners of money charge for lending out their money; it compensates them for time preference and the risk of inflation

Money is a commodity and, like all commodities, only earns when it is made to grow. If it is only hidden under the mattress, it may remain safe and retain its nominal value, but it will never earn anything extra. It is only when it is put out to work that it can grow in value and produce an income for the owner. The rent or charge for borrowing money and the income from lending money is interest. There are two types of interest, simple interest and compound interest. These are covered in more detail in Sections 3.1 and 3.2.

3.1   Simple Interest

Learning Objective 2.3.1

Know how to calculate: simple interest and Annual Percentage Rate (APR)

Simple interest occurs when interest is only paid on the basic sum borrowed. For example, assume you borrow £100 for one year at 5% per annum (pa). At the end of the year, you pay back £105, being £100 for the original capital sum and £5 for the interest. The simple interest makes no account of any charges or the effect of interest being charged at various intervals (e.g. daily, monthly or quarterly) over the period of the loan. It is the "quoted rate" but is only a base for further calculation whenever charges or periodic additions of interest are involved.

However, the quoted rate can be highly misleading unless full account is taken of both extra charges and how interest is charged.

Example

If charges or fees are added, this will increase the cost of the loan. Say a loan of £1,000 for one year is arranged, with an interest rate of 5% pa, paid at the end of the loan period and an arrangement fee of £25. At the end of the year, the borrower will pay back:

Capital sum	£1,000
Interest @ 5% (1000x5/100)	£50
Arrangement fee	£25
Total	£1,075

To compare against other loans, the borrower needs the annual percentage rate where the total cost of the loan, £75, is turned into a percentage rate that can be compared. The sum here is 75/1000x100 = 7.5%

3.2 Compound Interest

Learning Objective 2.3.2

Know how to calculate Annual Equivalent Rate (AER)

Compound interest occurs when interest is paid on interest as in the following example.

Example

£1,000 is borrowed for six months at a rate of 10% pa, payable monthly (interest rates are generally quoted at an annual rate, no matter what length of time the money is borrowed for). The monthly interest rate that is added to the loan is the annual rate of 10% divided by the 12 months in the year = 10%/12 = 0.833%.

Date	Opening balance (£)	Interest (£)	Closing balance (£)
End of month 1	1,000.00	8.33	1,008.33
End of month 2	1,008.33	8.40	1,016.74
End of month 3	1,016.74	8.47	1,025.21
End of month 4	1,025.21	8.54	1,033.75
End of month 5	1,033.75	8.61	1,042.36
End of month 6	1,042.36	8.68	1,051.04

Had the interest only been payable at the end of the six months, it would have been £50. Because it was payable monthly, interest has accrued not only on the £1,000 capital sum but also on the interest that has been added each month with the result that an extra £1.04 of interest has been paid.

£1.04 may not seem a great deal extra but the passage of time makes a major difference to the interest paid. Imagine that 100 years ago, your ancestor made two deposits of £1,000 and the bank with whom he made the deposit has just notified you that you are the beneficiary and can spend the money. On both deposits, the interest rate was 5% pa, payable annually. The first deposit has become £6,000, that is the original £1,000 plus £50 x 100 (£5,000) where the interest had been paid into a separate non-interest paying account. However, the second deposit, where the interest was credited to the same account, would have become £125,239.29 due to the magic of compound interest. There is no question as to which account has been the better investment.

It is therefore sensible to ensure that compound interest never works against you if you can possibly help it. If you borrow money, always ensure that at least the interest is paid off. If you permit interest to be charged on interest, it becomes much more difficult to pay off the debt. This is particularly the case where an expensive type of credit is being used, such as a credit card or a payday loan. It is like trying to run up the down escalator. It can be done, but only at the expense of an immense amount of extra effort.

3.3 Real Interest Rates

Financial papers are inclined to quote real interest rates. These show the rate paid on a loan or received on a deposit after taking inflation into account. If you are paying 5% on a loan and inflation is running at 2%, then you are paying a real interest rate of 3%. Although the money you have borrowed is earning interest, its value is dropping at the same time. Equally, if you are earning 1% on a deposit and inflation is running at the same 2%, in real terms the value of your money is actually dropping by 1% a year, net of the interest you have earned.

3.4 Calculating Interest Rates

When borrowing money, it is normal for the lender to charge interest. The lender might be a bank, a credit card company or even a payday loan company. The way the interest rate is disclosed could potentially be rather misleading.

Here are some fictional examples:

Example

Tom is looking to borrow some money to buy a new laptop; he has found four alternative sources:

1. *ABC bank is offering a loan that will charge interest at 10% per annum, with the interest being added to the loan each quarter.*
2. *XYZ bank is offering a loan that will charge interest at 10% per annum, with the interest being added to the loan each month.*
3. *The MISA credit card will charge interest at 1% each month.*
4. *The Payday Loan Company will charge interest at 1% each day.*

Which is the cheapest source of finance for Tom?

On a superficial basis, the two 1% quotes (the credit card and the payday loan) seem cheaper than the 10% quotes from the banks. However, it is pretty clear that the payday loan is the most expensive despite only quoting 1%, because the 1% is a daily rate. It can immediately be calculated as more like 365% per annum (as there are 365 days most years).

Similarly, but nowhere near as excessively, the MISA credit card looks expensive compared to the two banks. The banks are both quoting 10% and a monthly charge of 1% can immediately be thought of as around 12% per annum, as there are 12 months in each year.

So Tom is left with the choice of ABC or XYZ, each quoting 10%. However, there is a clear winner here – ABC Bank is cheaper because it charges interest every quarter, whereas XYZ adds it every month. This means that the balance on the loan increases every month at XYZ Bank but only every quarter at ABC Bank. Interest is charged on the outstanding balance, so, in effect, interest is being charged on interest more frequently at XYZ Bank. This is shown below if we assume Tom borrows £1,000 and we look at how the balance on the loan increases in the two banks over the first six months.

ABC Bank

The quarterly interest rate that is added to the loan is the annual rate of 10% divided by the four quarters in the year = 10%/4 = 2.5%.

Date	Opening balance (£)	Interest (£)	Closing balance (£)
End of month 1	1,000.00	–	1,000.00
End of month 2	1,000.00	–	1,000.00
End of month 3	1,000.00	25.00	1,025.00
End of month 4	1,025.00	–	1,025.00
End of month 5	1,025.00	–	1,025.00
End of month 6	1,025.00	25.625	1,050.625

XYZ Bank

The monthly interest rate that is added to the loan is the annual rate of 10% divided by the 12 months in the year = 10%/12 = 0.833%.

Date	Opening balance (£)	Interest (£)	Closing balance (£)
End of month 1	1,000.00	8.33	1,008.33
End of month 2	1,008.33	8.40	1,016.74
End of month 3	1,016.74	8.47	1,025.21
End of month 4	1,025.21	8.54	1,033.75
End of month 5	1,033.75	8.61	1,042.36
End of month 6	1,042.36	8.68	1,051.04

So, after six months it is clear from the above that ABC Bank is cheaper, with a loan balance of £1,050.625 compared to the larger loan balance of £1,051.04 at XYZ. This is because ABC is charging interest less frequently (quarterly compared to XYZ's monthly).

The above example shows that the way interest is disclosed can be misleading, unless care is taken to ensure that everything is taken into account. In reality, the regulatory authorities help too by requiring lenders to quote rates on a comparable basis. Quoted percentages have to be presented as annual figures and, lenders are also required to disclose some form of **annual equivalent rate (AER)**. The annual equivalent rate takes the quoted APR and adjusts it to take into account the frequency of interest charges. If the frequency of charging interest is annually, the quoted rates and AER rates are the same. When interest is charged more frequently than annually – for example quarterly, or monthly – the AER will be greater than the APR percentage.

Below is the detail from the earlier example presented with both the quoted rates and AER that makes the cheapest option much more straightforward to identify.

Example

Lender and detail	Quoted (per annum)	AER
ABC Bank – interest 10% per annum, each quarter	10%	10.38%
XYZ Bank – interest 10% per annum, each month	10%	10.47%
MISA credit card – interest at 1% each month	12%	12.68%
Payday Loan Company – interest at 1% each day	365%	3,678%

As the table shows, the quoted percentage begins to identify the more expensive options immediately, particularly the Payday Loan Company's 365%. However, it is the AER that shows just how expensive the payday loan is compared to all of the others at well over 3,000%! The AER also clearly shows that the ABC Bank option is the cheapest, since, despite having the same quoted percentage as XYZ Bank, the interest is charged less frequently.

In summary, when comparing the cost of borrowing, it is sensible to:

* look at the annual quoted rate rather than quarterly, monthly weekly or daily percentages;
* look for the AER to make a true comparison, including the impact of how often the interest is charged.

4. Types and Costs of Borrowing

Learning Objective 2.4

Know that banks and other financial institutions offer many different borrowing products to individuals

Banks and other financial institutions offer many different ways of borrowing money to individuals, companies and, indeed, governments. These reflect the requirements of the borrower, how long the money is required for, whether it is secured on assets and the financial status of the borrower. All these considerations will influence the ability of the borrower to obtain funds and the cost of that borrowing.

4.1 Borrowing from Banks – Loans and Overdrafts

Learning Objective 2.4.1

Understand the difference between fixed-term loans and overdrafts, which can be withdrawn at any time

A loan from the bank is generally inflexible, but you know where you stand when entering in to a loan agreement. So long as the borrower keeps to the terms agreed at the start of the loan, the bank not only will not but cannot change the terms or ask for the money back unexpectedly. Loans are usually taken out for a specific purpose such as the purchase of an asset, for example a car, or to repay debts incurred elsewhere, such as on credit cards. They will have an agreed repayment schedule and a fixed interest rate. Of course, if the borrower fails to keep to the terms, the bank can demand repayment in full or impose more onerous terms.

Overdrafts, on the other hand, are a flexible facility that the borrower can use as required. Within an agreed limit, the borrower can draw down (ie, borrow) and repay as he or she wishes. It is often used for funds at the end of a month, to allow financial opportunities to be taken or just to ensure that an unexpected requirement for funds does not cause embarrassment. Overdrafts are frequently offered to students, interest free, as part of the package banks use to gain the business of potentially good long-term customers, given that customers will often get remarried sooner than they change their bank!

- However, when a customer borrows funds without the agreement of the bank, these are called unauthorised overdrafts and the charging structure reflects the lack of agreement. There may be no agreement at all or the customer may borrow more than the agreed limit without asking the bank first. It is always best to ask the bank first and get its agreement if there is the possibility that the limit may be exceeded, if only to reduce the fees the bank may charge.
- The bank always has the option of withdrawing the overdraft facility without notice and requiring any borrowing to be repaid. This is the downside of the overdraft facility, but the bank usually only withdraws an overdraft when it has a good reason for acting in this way, such as fearing that it may not get its money back if it lets the facility continue or because the customer has abused the facility.

4.2 Secured and Unsecured Borrowing

Learning Objective 2.4.3

Borrowers can offer to the lender a valuable possession (ie, an asset) as security that the loan will be repaid. A mortgage is a loan secured on the property being purchased

The funds being borrowed may be secured by giving the bank a charge over the borrower's assets. The most favoured asset, from the bank's point of view, is the customer's house. Giving a charge means that the bank can sell the asset if the borrower fails to repay the loan as agreed, without making the customer bankrupt. Other forms of security can be the borrower's investments, such as a share portfolio, or a guarantee. A guarantee is when

someone connected (it may be a friend or relation) promises to repay the debt if the actual borrower fails to do so.

When the borrower is a private company without assets, the bank will usually require the directors and shareholders to guarantee the company's debt and may demand a charge over the directors' houses to support it. From the bank's point of view, this not only gives it added security if things go wrong but also ensures that the directors are fully focussed on making the company profitable.

If the bank does not ask for security, such borrowing is known as **unsecured**. This means that should the customer fail to repay, the bank will have to make the customer bankrupt, in which case any assets are shared out equally amongst all the creditors. This increases the risk to the bank that it will not get all the money it lent back.

The charging structure of the facility will always reflect the presence or absence of security. An unsecured facility, which can be a loan or an overdraft, will always be more expensive than a secured one, and usually significantly so.

The most usual form of secured borrowing for non-business purposes is for house purchase where the loan is called a mortgage. The loan is secured on the property and if the borrower fails to keep up to date with payments, the lender, usually a bank or building society, can seize ownership of the property and sell it to repay the loan. If there is a surplus and there are no other creditors, this is paid to the borrower. However, if the proceeds of the house sale are insufficient to repay the loan, the UK borrower is still responsible for the balance, unlike in many states in the US where the borrower can hand over the keys and walk away with no further liability.

4.3 Other Sources of Finance

Learning Objective 2.4.2

Understand the characteristics of credit cards and pay-day loans; how outstanding balances can quickly build up

The better off and organised you are and the less you need to borrow, the cheaper it is. The broke and desperate can still find sources of finance but they will cost far more.

The most readily available form of borrowing, particularly for impulse purchases, is the credit card. It is convenient, accepted everywhere, offers a period of free credit and easy to obtain. However, once past the free credit period, it is expensive. Bank credit cards charge around 16% pa while store cards charge up to 30% pa. If the interest and some of the capital is not paid off each month, the magic of compound interest starts working against the borrower and paying off the debt becomes more difficult. Using cards to obtain the optimum benefit requires forethought and self-discipline, by ensuring that any balance is paid off before the end of any interest-free period.

Pawnbrokers are another form of borrowing that has flourished recently. Pawnbrokers demand a form of security by holding a possession of the borrower until the loan is repaid. Since the pawnbroker requires a possession that is portable and intrinsically valuable, the favoured security is the family jewellery. If the loan is not repaid, the pawnbroker will sell the security. Interest rates charged are usually higher than credit cards so the facility is used by those who find it difficult or impossible to raise more mainstream credit.

For the really desperate, there are payday loans. As the name implies, these are designed to bridge the gap between running out of money and the next payday. The interest rate for a week can be as high as 30%, which translates into an annual interest rate of 4,500%. With interest rates this high, it is too easy to fall into a vicious circle where the gap between running out of money and the next payday grows ever larger. Even considering such a facility should be a warning to seek help from the Citizens' Advice Bureau (CAB) or the debt advice charities.

4.4 Bonds

Learning Objective 2.4.5

Governments and large companies borrow money in return for IOUs called bonds. These loans are usually for large amounts and usually have a fixed term of several years' duration and carry a fixed rate of interest

Sizeable entities, such as governments and major companies borrow large sums and do so by issuing IOUs to the market. These are called bonds and are usually for a fixed interest rate and for a fixed term, though there are a number of different ways that a bond can be structured, depending on what the market wants and therefore what can be most easily sold. Bonds can be quoted on the stock market and can therefore be sold if the holder wants cash.

4.5   Other Costs for Loans

Learning Objective 2.4.4

Loans incur administration costs for lenders irrespective of the size of the loan: a loan for a large sum of money is therefore most cost effective for lenders, allowing them to offer an otherwise lower rate of interest to the borrower

Interest is the most obvious cost of any loan, but is not the only one. The issue of a loan incurs administration costs, even where computers take much of the burden, marketing costs, something to cover the cost of loans that are may not be repaid and extra costs loaded by complying with the regulations. Many of these are fixed, no matter what the size of the loan is and the lenders may try and recoup them either by increasing the interest rate or by charging initial fees.

If the lender offers a fixed rate for a term, such as a fixed rate mortgage, they will often borrow the money on a fixed rate too. If the borrower repays early (usually because it is possible to borrow elsewhere at a lower rate), the lender will still have to honour the rate it is paying for the deposit and will try to recoup this cost by charging an early repayment fee.

📑 Chapter Questions

Based on what you have learned in Chapter Two, try to answer the following questions.

Think of an answer for each question and refer to the appropriate section for confirmation.

1. Why is money now generally better than money in the future?

    Answer reference: Section 2.2

    ....

    ....

2. Explain the effects of inflation.

    Answer reference: Section 2.2

    ....

    ....

3. Why are falling prices in a deflationary situation not recommended?

    Answer reference: Section 2.3

    ....

    ....

4. Explain how compound interest works.

    Answer reference: Section 3.2

    ....

    ....

5. Why is a secured loan likely to be at a lower rate of interest than an unsecured loan?

    Answer reference: Section 4.2

    ....

    ....

CISI
CHARTERED INSTITUTE FOR
SECURITIES & INVESTMENT

Risk and Reward

1. Introduction   33

2. The Risks of Investment   35

3. The Rewards of Investment   38

4. The Relationship Between Risk and Reward   40

This syllabus area will provide approximately 3 of the 30 examination questions

Risk and Reward

1. Introduction

Learning Objective 3

People face financial risks in the course of their everyday lives. They also risk losing their money when they invest it. The level of risk varies according to the type of investment. The anticipated reward from making an investment should reflect the level of risk attached to it: the greater the risk, the greater the reward required by the investor to compensate for that risk

There is no such thing as a risk-free investment. Indeed, there is no such thing as a risk-free activity. Even walking down the street has a risk. This chapter is about understanding risk and how risk and reward balance out and how to guard against and mitigate risk. Understanding this allows you to guard against the risks and be better placed to enjoy the rewards.

1.1 Personal Financial Risks

Learning Objective 3.1

Individuals face financial risk in the everyday course of their lives

The risks described in the following sections may be rare, but they can be catastrophic when they do occur. While care can be taken, such as locking the door to keep burglars out, installing fire alarms, keeping fit in order to reduce risks, avoidance cannot be guaranteed. It therefore makes sense to take steps to reduce the impact, mainly through insurance.

Insurance guards against events that, it is hoped, will never happen, such as accidents. Assurance prepares for events that undoubtedly will happen, notably death.

1.2 Risk of Loss of Personal Assets

Learning Objective 3.1.1

Risk to personal assets, such as homes, household possessions and cars etc, from accidental damage, fire or theft

There are always risks associated with possessions, such as theft, fire and accident. The ownership of personal assets, of which property, cars and personal possessions (clothes, furniture, jewellery and valuables) are the most usual, brings with it pleasure and security but also responsibilities. The risks can be covered by insurance and this is described in detail in Chapter 4.

However, insurance is a contract that is covered by terms and conditions, better known as the small print. Apart from fulfilling the insurance company's legal requirements, the small print is there to protect the company and not the client. A major part of the small print describes how the company will not cover losses where the client has not fulfilled his responsibilities to take care of the assets. If the client (which is you) fails to take care of the asset and, because of that, the asset is lost or damaged, the company will not pay out some or all of the loss. If the door is left open for the thief, if the house is not maintained and the rain rots the roof, if the purse is left on the bench and stolen, then the company will not pay up, and rightly so, for possessions bring responsibilities.

1.3 The Risk of Loss of Earnings

Learning Objective 3.1.2

Risk to earnings from ill health, injury or accidental death

Buying or renting somewhere to live, feeding a family and buying possessions takes money and that money comes from having a job. If the job is lost through redundancy, illness or an accident, the income will no longer be paid into the bank account. Though the state will pay benefits, these will usually only replace a small part of the lost income. It is, however, possible to insure against losing a job. This type of insurance is known as income protection. In an income protection policy, the insurance company will pay a regular income, which will still be lower than that paid through employment, until a new job is found or the client reaches pensionable age. The amount of income protection necessary depends on the client's circumstances. A young person with no dependents is in a different situation from that of a parent with young children.

1.4 Third-Party Liability

Learning Objective 3.1.3

Causing third parties to suffer injury or death; causing damage to third parties' property

It is possible to become liable for the damage or financial loss suffered by a third party. The most common use of the phrase is probably in car insurance where the legal minimum insurance policy a car owner has to have is called third-party, fire and theft. This means that the insurance company will pay the damages of the person you crashed into but not pay to repair your car.

Although third-party liability is probably the most common with motor insurance, this is not the only situation. Most household insurance policies have third-party liability insurance, covering such situations as when visitors to the house suffer an accident through your fault, for instance, when they trip on the loose paving stone on your drive or the excellent cricket shot by your child breaks next door's window.

2. The Risks of Investment

Learning Objective 3.2

Any investment, from buying one's own home to buying shares in a company, carries additional risks

There is no such thing as a risk-free investment. Moreover, the risk attached to any investment will change over time and needs to be regularly monitored. Changes in the world economy, in

fiscal and monetary policy, in technology and in social fashion can all impact on how profitable an investment may be. Even property, probably the most profitable generally held investment of the last half century in the UK, has suffered periods of time and geographical areas where owning a house has been disastrous for the owner.

The most usual forms of investments for most people, and probably for most readers of this workbook, over their lifetime, are cash, property, bonds and shares. There are, of course, many other investments such as commodities, gold, antiques, racehorses, modern first editions of books, postage stamps and cars. In fact, there are surprisingly few things that have never been regarded as an investment by someone. The risks regarding these include the same ones that cover the first four, cash, property, bonds and shares, together with others peculiar to each form of investment. These unusual types of investment are best left to those with an interest in and a specialised knowledge of them, and generally the wealth to indulge their interest.

FTSE 100 Share Index

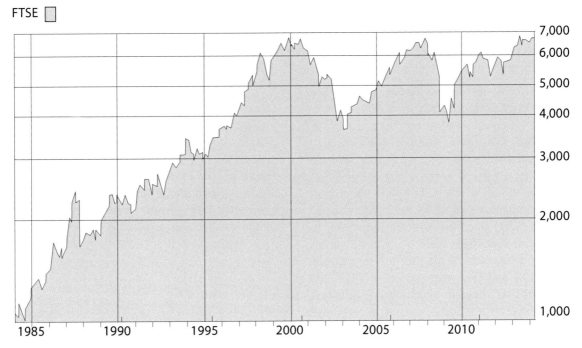

Source: Yahoo! UK & Ireland 28 April 2014

Figure 4

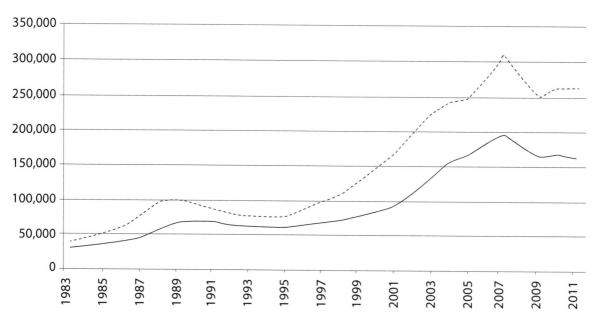

House Prices in the UK and London 1983 – 2011

—— UK House Prices

– – – London House Prices

Source: Monevator.com

Figure 5

2.1 Price and Value Risk

Learning Objective 3.2.1

The price of financial assets and other assets (such as property) can fall

All advertisements for investments are now legally obliged to contain a warning that prices can fall as well as rise and that fact should always be borne in mind when making an investment. However, with risk comes opportunity. Figure 4 is the chart a the FTSE 100 share index, a composite of the hundred largest companies quoted on the London Stock Exchange (LSE) since it first started in 1984. It can be seen that there have been three major setbacks: the 1987 crash, the dot com crash of 2000–01 and the financial crash of 2007. In spite of that, anyone investing in the index in 1984 would have increased his investment sevenfold in spite of the setbacks. It is an old investment saying that it is time, not timing, that is important. In other words, it is usually better to stay invested than it is to try and

be clever and guess what the market is going to do. Having said that, it is also a regulatory requirement that advertising material that quotes historic performance must warn that the past is not necessarily a guide to the future.

2.2 Gearing

Gearing occurs when an investment is purchased using borrowed money. For most people, this will only happen when buying a property – a house to live in. Looking at the house purely as an investment (which in real life, it very rarely is) any move in the value of the house has a much greater impact on the family wealth, due to gearing.

For instance, assume that you buy a flat for £100,000. This is made up of £90,000 from a mortgage and a £10,000 deposit from your savings. If the value of the flat increases by 20% to £120,000, your share has tripled to £30,000 and you start to feel comfortably richer! However, if the value falls by 20% to £80,000, not only has your deposit been wiped out but you are in **negative equity** as you still owe the bank £90,000 but your asset (your flat) is worth £10,000 less than the debt. The bank will not throw you out while you continue to pay the agreed regular repayment but your financial position has become much more precarious and you might need a recovery in property prices to rescue you.

As you can see from Figure 5 above, in the long term, houses have been a spectacular investment but a closer look reveals that there have been periods when they have not, from 1990 to 1995 and from 2007 to 2009.

2.3 Liquidity Risk

Learning Objective 3.2.2

Liquidity means the ease with which an investment can be converted back into cash. It may be difficult to convert an investment into cash if the market has insufficient buyers and sellers (ie, it is illiquid)

A liquid investment is one where there are sufficient buyers and sellers to guarantee that you can always sell it if the cash is required. Liquidity varies not only between different types of investment but also within the same class of investment depending on size, economic climate, attractiveness and other qualities peculiar to that particular investment.

Shares quoted on the LSE or, indeed, any of the world's major stock exchanges, are generally regarded as liquid investments where you can get your money back within a matter of days. However, even here liquidity varies markedly. On the London Stock Exchange each company share is given a figure for NMS. NMS stands for Normal Market Size and this is the maximum number of shares that a market maker guarantees to deal in at the price quoted. This figure varies depending on the size of the company involved. For the very largest companies, such as Shell or Vodafone, the normal market size may be as high as 500,000 shares. For companies at the other end of the spectrum, investors may struggle to buy more than 500 shares at a time. The bigger the NMS, the more liquid the share is.

Cash is the most liquid investment, unless the investor falls foul of the money laundering regulations. You will never find difficulty in getting rid of a £20 note. Property, however, varies considerably. When the market is strong, a nice house in a good area can sell at the asking price within 24 hours of going on the market. On the other hand, there are whole streets in some former mining villages in parts of the UK empty and boarded up, as there are no buyers at any price.

2.4 Delivery Risk

This is not a risk that affects most people. If you buy a new chair from John Lewis, you can expect it to be delivered as promised. However, it is a risk at the heart of how markets work and was the risk most feared by governments and central bankers in the 2007 financial crash. Market operators rely on the delivery of what they have purchased. However, each transaction can be one of a long string of transactions, stretching round the globe, and it only takes one failure in that string not only to act like removing a card from the base of a house of cards, but also to undermine the creditworthiness of all the participants. The actions of governments in the most recent financial crash were aimed at insuring that the failure of any one participant, such as Northern Rock, did not bring the entire banking system crashing down. In this they were largely successful, but at a huge cost to taxpayers.

2.5 Issuer/Default Risk

Learning Objective 3.2.3

The company that issues shares or bonds (or the bank or building society that accepts deposits) might go into liquidation and be unable to repay investors in full

There is always the possibility that the asset invested in may become valueless. In the case of shares and bonds, this happens when the company issuing them becomes insolvent. In this situation, the company is put into liquidation, the assets are sold off and the proceeds distributed in strict order of preference. First are the secured creditors are paid off with the proceeds from the assets on which they held mortgages. Then the unsecured creditors, which will include trade creditors, the tax authorities and bond holders will be paid off equally for each pound owed. If there is anything left, a most unusual experience, this is paid equally to the shareholders per share held.

3. The Rewards of Investment

Learning Objective 3.3

Investment is rewarded in three main ways: interest; dividend and capital gain. Sometimes it can be a combination of more than one of these types of reward

Investment is rewarded in three ways – income, which can be in the form of interest, rent or dividends, and capital gain. Income and capital gain are not mutually exclusive and investors can enjoy both rewards from the same investment. However, there are investments which are aimed at only one of these. There are shares which pay no dividends and investors rely on capital growth for their reward. Annuities, which are explained in more detail in Chapter 9, Section 3, only produce income, with the capital being lost at the end of the term.

The rewards of investment not only compensate the investor for not spending the money for more immediate gratification but also for the risk

inherent in the investment. The investor expects to benefit more from saving and investing than from spending the money immediately.

3.1 Interest

Learning Objective 3.3.1

Interest compensates the owner of the money for: not being able to spend it on other things immediately; for future erosion of the value of the money by inflation; for the risk that the money might not be repaid

Interest is paid on debt. The debt may be a deposit with a bank, a loan to a company in the form of a bond, a loan to the government in the shape of government stock or national savings bonds or a loan to a friend or relative. Generally, interest is fixed at an agreed rate but it may be according to an agreed formula, such as, say, 2% over base rate. Base rate is the rate at which the Bank of England will lend to other banks when they require assistance. Some Government stocks pay a rate that is increased each year by the rate of inflation, as measured by the Retail Price Index.

The real interest rate paid is the rate left after taking inflation into account and is the net benefit to the investor. If the investor receives an interest rate of 3% and inflation is 2%, then the real interest rate is 1%. However, if the investor is paid 1% and inflation is still 2%, the real interest rate is a negative –1%. In other words, the investor is not receiving sufficient to compensate him for the loss of buying power.

3.2 Dividends

Learning Objective 3.3.2

Shareholders receive a return on the capital they invest in companies in the form of dividends – a proportionate share of the company's distributed profits

The income received from investment in shares is called **dividends**. Companies can pay dividends out of the profit the company makes. Each share will receive the same amount. By law, a company can only pay dividends out of profits that it has made, either in that year or out of profits it has made in previous years but not paid out. The ideal company from an income point of view is one that increases its profits and dividend at a steady rate every year. This is difficult to do and very few companies can claim to have increased dividends every year over a long period of, say, 40 years.

3.3   Rent

Rent is paid for the hire of property, whether that property be a house for living in, a shop, farmland, industrial premises or any other landed asset. Long-term rents usually have a clause allowing the landlord, the owner of the property, to increase the rent on a regular basis, such as every five years. This is always subject to negotiation and the tenant, who hires or rents the property, has the option of walking away and finding somewhere else at a cheaper rate. Since good long-term tenants are valuable, the landlord may consider it wise to charge less than he could get if he were to put the property on the open market, where he may get a tenant who pays a higher rent initially but then fails to maintain the payments.

3.4   Capital Gain

Learning Objective 3.3.3

Capital gain results from an increase in the market value of the investment

A capital gain is made when the value of the asset increases and the asset is then sold. Until the asset is sold the gain is only potential and a change in circumstances or in the market may turn the profit into a loss. The benefit of a capital gain is that it can be far greater than interest obtainable on a similar sum. A suddenly successful product, a change of fashion or market sentiment can send a company's share price soaring. In 1969, Poseidon, an Australian mining company, announced that it had found nickel in the Australian outback. The shares moved from 50p to £120 in a matter of weeks and sparked a scramble for other shares in what was known as the Australian nickel boom.

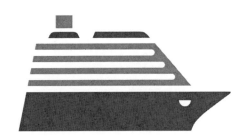

The fact that the example quoted dates from 1969 should warn the reader how rare it is to make a fortune this way. One of a large bank's stock exchange advisory departments used to comment that investing in a speculative share was only better than betting on the favourite in the 2.30 horse race at Newbury because the excitement lasted rather longer but that the result was too often the same – the loss of the investment!

However, prudent investing, following good advice and doing homework can enable good gains in investing over the long term. It follows that only money that can be lost without catastrophically affecting a family's finances and which is not needed for other more urgent purposes, such as eating, should be used for long-term investing.

A commonly heard phrase is that the house is regarded as the pension fund. A good house with no mortgage can be used as a source of funds in later life, either through trading down or equity release, the term used for borrowing against the value of the house. Care should be taken with either of these options. Saving and investment, ensuring that inflation and compound interest work in your favour, are still most often thought to be the best way to plan for your future.

4. The Relationship Between Risk and Reward

Learning Objective 3.4

Lenders (and investors) will always seek higher returns to compensate them for higher risk

Risk and reward are closely entwined opposites. It is difficult, if not impossible, to have one without the other. The accepted rule is that the higher the risk of loss, the higher the potential reward. Much investment research is dedicated to finding investments where the market's judgement on the risk or the potential return is wrong. This is, of course, easier to establish with hindsight when commenting on past market movements but is highly profitable when the foresight is correct.

4.1 Mitigating Risk and Improving Reward

These two aspects of investment, and, indeed, of life in general, are the two sides of the same coin. Those who study and understand the risks and how to reduce them where they cannot be avoided are most likely to achieve successful outcomes. Both business and finance require work to understand the risks before becoming involved and then ensuring constantly keeping up to date in order to avoid being caught out by changes in the economy, regulation or technology.

4.2 Long-Term and Short-Term Investments

Learning Objective 3.4.1

The longer money is tied up in an investment, the greater the chance that something can go wrong. This will be reflected in a higher return being offered to the investor

The marketing material for any stock-market based investment vehicle is likely to have a clause in it, stating that you should only invest if you can leave the money invested for at least

five years. A look at figure 4 indicates that such a term is required to enjoy growth in the economy or recover from the setbacks. It is an old stock exchange joke that a long-term investment is a short-term speculation that went wrong. The history of the last century has shown that time is a great healer of mistakes and, while the regulations state that the past should never be taken as a guide to the future, so far, that has been the way to bet.

However, there are investors who are called day traders in the stock exchange who invest very short-term, looking to exploit short term movements. Much of their activity is based on the study of charts and requires full-time involvement and the backing of substantial cash reserves but is profitable for the successful. The unsuccessful tend to leave the market rapidly.

4.3 Long-Term and Short-Term Deposits

The longer the term of the deposit, the higher it is likely that the interest rate payable will be. Both lender and borrower benefit from the security and convenience of a longer-term agreement and this is reflected in the higher interest rate. However, there are risks for both parties. Apart from the possibility that the financial position of the deposit taker may change for the worse, interest rates may move against either party or the lender may find that it would have been more profitable to have had a deposit on a shorter term. If interest rates rise in the meantime, the depositor might be able to increase the interest income achievable whilst the deposit taker could have found it more profitable to borrow shorter term had interest rates fallen.

4.4 Diversification versus Concentration

Diversification – the spread of investment – is covered in greater depth later. It is considered to be one of the ways of reducing the risk of investment, in that if one of the investments in a portfolio crashes, it will only be a small part of the total invested.

An alternative theory of investment advocates concentration, and states that you should put all your eggs in one basket and watch it like a hawk. This method of investing is only recommended when the investor knows exactly what he is doing and is prepared to put the time and energy into keeping a very close eye on what is happening to his investment.

4.5 Credit Ratings

Learning Objective 3.4.2

Borrowers (and issuers of shares) are rated by outside agencies for their credit-worthiness. The lower their credit-rating, the higher the risk they will default. The higher the risk of default, the higher the interest rate (or dividend) they will have to offer

Borrowers, from governments to the smallest companies, are studied by outside agencies for their credit-worthiness and marked accordingly, depending on the judgement of the agency. Credit ratings range from AAA to junk, with the former being considered undoubted and the latter considered likely to fail and be unable to repay their debts. This judgement is reflected in the interest rates that each is likely to pay and the ease with which they can raise finance. Since very few companies do not borrow in some way, the ratings are also used for assessing the value of the shares issued by the company.

It must be emphasised that the ratings are purely the opinion of the company rating them and that rating agencies can and do make errors. This was revealed in the financial crash of 2007 when some companies, particularly Lehman Bros, a major US banking house, went from AAA to failure practically overnight. This has resulted in the credit agencies being more cautious in their judgement.

4.6 Personal Credit Ratings

Learning Objective 3.4.3

Individuals build up a credit history, based on past borrowing and repayment patterns. People with poor credit histories have to pay much higher interest rates than people with good credit scores

While companies are judged on their balance sheets, individuals are judged on their credit history. Lenders' experiences with individual borrowers are collated by central agencies. Together with court records and other available reports, these are used by banks and other lenders as a basis for making judgements on whether to grant credit. Those with good credit histories can usually borrow on preferential terms while those who have failed to repay debt in the past are likely to find it difficult to borrow in the future or maybe condemned to borrowing from payday lenders at very high rates of interest.

Individuals are entitled, under the regulations, to request copies of their credit history from the central agencies, that cost £2, and can correct mistakes that may have arisen. They can also use the information to judge the likelihood of receiving credit at a rate that makes it worthwhile.

4.7 Secured versus Unsecured Lending

Learning Objective 3.4.4

A loan secured on an asset, such as a house or flat, is less risky than an unsecured loan like an outstanding credit card balance. The interest rate will therefore usually be lower

Lenders use the information from credit agencies to decide on their willingness to grant credit. However, one of the other factors in lenders' decisions is the availability of security. As seen earlier, security is an asset of the borrower that the lender can sell to repay the debt, if the borrower fails to keep to the terms of the agreement. The most usual form of security is the borrower's home, particularly when the loan is a mortgage to buy the property. However, there are many forms of assets that lenders might accept as security against a loan, such as share portfolios, cars or the guarantee of a credit-worthy third party, such as a parent, relative or friend.

A secured loan is likely to be at a lower rate of interest than an unsecured loan, since the lender will have more confidence that the loan will be repaid.

📝 Chapter Questions

Based on what you have learned in Chapter Three, try to answer the following questions.

Think of an answer for each question and refer to the appropriate section for confirmation.

1. Explain the risks and rewards of equity investment.

   Answer reference: Sections 2.1, 3.2 and 3.4

   ....

   ....

2. What are the differences between liquidity risk, delivery risk and default risk?

   Answer reference: Sections 2.3, 2.4 and 2.5

   ....

   ....

3. Explain how personal credit ratings affect a customer's ability to borrow.

   Answer reference: Section 4.5

   ....

4. How do the rewards on deposits differ from those on shares?

   Answer reference: Section 3

   ....

   ....

Protection from Risks

1. Introduction   47

2. Diversification   49

3. Collective Investment   51

4. Syndication   52

This syllabus area will provide approximately 3 of the 30 examination questions

Protection from Risks

1. Introduction

Learning Objective 4

Individuals and other investors can take steps to protect themselves from risk

Individuals and companies can protect themselves from the financial results of risks. Protection from the physical results comes from taking care and is not a subject for this workbook.

1.1 Insurance and Insurance Companies

Learning Objective 4.1

Insurance is a way of transferring risk from individuals and firms to others – usually insurance companies

The theory behind insurance is that the event (car crash, theft, fire, accident) is comparatively rare but can be catastrophic to those who suffer it. Say that one person in a thousand has an accident. There is no telling in advance which one of the thousand is going to be the one that suffers. However, if each one of the thousand pays a relatively modest sum into a fund, there will be enough money available to offset the financial results of the accident to the one who does suffer it.

Insurance companies started as mutual help societies providing assistance and protection. You can still see the insurance badges on some old houses, placed there so that the private fire services knew which fires it was their responsibility to put out and which should be left to other insurance companies' fire services. They are now major companies, many trading worldwide and covering all types of risk while others specialise in one industry.

1.2 Insurance Premiums

Learning Objective 4.1.1
Individuals pay fees called insurance premiums in return for a guarantee that they will be compensated for a specific loss – such as the theft of their car

The fee paid for insurance cover is called a premium. Ideally, all the premiums paid for a certain risk over the period of cover, usually a year, will cover all the compensation that the insurance company has to pay, while leaving a margin to cover administration and profit. If the company miscalculates the degree of risk and the premiums paid fail to cover the compensation required, for instance, if an oil rig catches fire in the Gulf of Mexico, the insurance company will make a loss and will have to use reserves from profits made in previous years to ensure that all the compensation due is paid. Moreover, if competition in the industry means that the insurance company is unable to charge the premiums it considers necessary to cover the risk it may need to take a loss just to ensure that business continues to come in and boost their other source of profit–insurance funds.

1.3 Insurance Funds

Learning Objective 4.1.2
Insurers collect these premiums together in a pool of money and use it to pay out compensation for insured losses. They try to ensure that the fund is always sufficient to cover any losses

Insurance companies create a pool of money made up of all of the premiums paid by customers. This pool of money is then used to pay out compensation to those customers making a successful claim. Insurance companies work on the basis that premiums will be paid and are available for investment before compensation has to be paid out. These premiums are paid into the company's investment funds and invested in the money market and stock market to make a profit and add to the company's reserves, available to cover any unforeseen disasters or miscalculations in the level of premiums that should be charged. Given that the time lag between the payment of the premium, something happening that means compensation has to be paid and the time that the insurance company actually pays out is usually quite long and can be a matter of years, the pool of money can be substantial. Once again, the magic of big numbers works in the insurance company's favour, in that the profit margin on each individual transaction can be small but still mount up when consolidated together. Insurance companies try to ensure that the fund is always sufficient to cover any losses.

1.4 The Relationship between Insurance Premiums and Risk

Learning Objective 4.1.3
The higher the risk of a loss occurring, the higher the premium the insurance company will wish to charge

As already seen, insurance companies plan to cover the compensation payable, administration costs and profit with the premiums they charge. The companies use a vast body of knowledge in calculating what level of premium to charge. Looking, for instance, at house insurance in the UK, the insurance companies have experience dating back many years and in some instances, centuries. The Sun Fire Office (part of RSA plc) dates back to 1710 while Scottish Widows was founded in 1815. The use of technology, and in particular computerised databases, allows the companies to estimate what the level of risk is for each particular house. The companies will look at the level of crime in the area, the possibility of flooding and subsidence and even the house holder's history of making claims when deciding what premium to charge. If they consider that the householder is unlikely to make a claim, for whatever reason, the company will be happy to make a very competitive quote for the premium. On the other hand, for a potential customer that they consider to be high risk, with a claim record that indicates a readiness to claim even where the insurance company suspects that the customer is not always as truthful as the insurance company would like, then the quote is likely to be raised to uncompetitive levels, in the hope that the customer goes elsewhere.

The greater willingness of customers to claim, whether justifiably or fraudulently is an increasingly important factor in deciding the level of premium to quote. According to industry spokesmen, the level of exaggerated or, indeed, plainly fraudulent claims has raised the overall cost of car insurance by around 25% in the UK. For instance, whiplash is extremely painful for those who have suffered it but it is extremely difficult to prove one way or the other since it relies on the sufferer's word. The insurance industry may be very cynical about the level of claims that they see but find it difficult to do anything but pay out and charge all policyholders for higher premiums than might otherwise be the case.

The marketplace ensures that the premium reflects the risk and is not too profitable. If a line of business becomes too profitable, other companies will enter the market at a lower price. The competition might mean that premiums, in due course, become too low and the industry starts making a loss, at which point the weaker competitors leave the market, supply and demand balance out and those remaining in the market can raise prices and become profitable again. At this point, new competitors enter the market and the price of premiums starts falling again as the insurance cycle repeats itself.

2. Diversification

Learning Objective 4.2

Just as individuals and firms can spread their risk with the help of an insurance company, investors can spread their risk by investing across many different types of investment or different geographical markets

The point of insurance is to provide compensation should a potentially catastrophic action occur. Diversification – a spread of interests – means that a setback in one area is prevented from being catastrophic by expansion in other areas. While concentrating activity or investment in only one or in very few areas means that expansion could have an exaggerated effect on the investor's wealth, a setback can bankrupt the investor. Spreading investment means that growth is less dramatic but so are setbacks.

The principal of diversification obviously works for manufacturing or service companies which can expand into different types of activities. However, this chapter and, indeed, this workbook concentrates on investment diversification.

2.1 Diversification across Different Types of Investment

Learning Objective 4.2.1

Financial service providers can help investors identify a range of suitable investments, such as shares, bonds, property or commodities like gold. These are known as asset classes

There are a number of different types of investment, some more mainstream than others. Cash, property, bonds and shares are the key asset classes that make up most UK portfolios, with possibly some of the more risky options included for a small part of the portfolio for fun – vintage cars for example. The emphasis will change as the appetite for risk and the economic outlook change. Over a lifetime the ability to take a risky position changes. When young, saving for a house and possibly still burdened by student loans, certainty is both required and prudent, and even more so when the expense of children arrives. As the children become self-supporting, often at a time when the salary has risen to reflect age and experience, it is possible to become more venturesome in investment outlook. With retirement, the emphasis on caution returns. So, over a lifetime, the risk preference will move from safer investments like cash to more risky investments like equity and back to safety again.

It is not necessary to invest directly into individual holdings in the various asset classes. This may be difficult as there are often investment minimums, particularly for bonds and property, which are beyond the reach of most modest investors. There are investment vehicles available which allow investment backed by expert advice and management at a modest cost and in modest amounts. These are described below in Section 3 of this chapter.

2.2 Geographical Diversification

Learning Objective 4.2.2

The economies of countries around the world experience different rates of growth: financial advisers can help investors spread their investments across different geographic markets to reduce the risk of being overly exposed to one particular market

As with spreading investment across different asset classes, it is also possible to invest across the world. Different countries and even different continents can have different rates of growth. The arguments for diversification made for different asset classes above apply equally to spreading investment across the world. Since it is virtually impossible to monitor an overseas market without being closely involved and preferably being located in that country, it is best to invest through an investment fund that

specialises in the target market. Diversifying geographically not only can increase the chances of growth but it can also reduce the risk of being overly exposed to one particular market.

2.3 Portfolio Investment

Learning Objective 4.2.3

With the help of professional advice, investors build up a portfolio of investments with an overall risk profile with which they feel comfortable

As soon as an investor has investments, he has a portfolio which has to be monitored and managed. If the investor has the expertise, the time and the interest, he can do this himself. However, most investors put their money into investments and forget about it, also forgetting that the reasons for purchase either fulfil themselves or never actually happen. In both these cases, the investment needs to be reviewed as to whether it still fulfils the purpose behind its purchase.

As well as reviewing the individual investments, it is necessary to review the purpose and profile of the portfolio as a whole. Purposes change, if only because circumstances change. It is pointless still saving for the children's education if they have all left school and are earning successfully.

3. Collective Investment

Learning Objective 4.3

Small investors with insufficient money to spread across many different investments can 'pool' their money with other investors' money in collective investment schemes

We have already seen in Section One of this Chapter how insurance works by mutual association as many customers seeking insurance cover work together to reduce the cost and increase flexibility. The same principle works in investment. Mutual funds were set up in the US and first came to the UK in 1931. These funds are called unit trusts in the UK and they are open-ended funds. There is no limit to the number of units that can be bought by investors as extra units can be created to meet demand. Units are purchased from the manager of the trust by investors or sold back to the manager when the investor wants his money back. The manager calculates the price on each dealing day (usually each working day) by dividing the total value of the fund by the number of units issued.

A number of other collective investment schemes (CIS) have joined unit trusts on the market. The most notable are OEICs (open ended investment companies) and ETFs (exchange-traded funds). The differences are mainly technical and regulatory but from the point of view of the investor, they do the same job in much the same way.

Another form of collective investment scheme is the investment trust, which predates unit trusts by a considerable margin. The first investment trust, Foreign and Colonial, which is still in existence, was founded in 1868. Investment trusts are closed-ended funds. In other words, there are a fixed number of shares available and these are purchased in the stock market. The price is dictated like that of any share by the balance between purchasers and sellers. As a result, the share price may be above (at a premium to) or below (at a discount to) the value of the underlying assets.

All collective investment schemes work in much the same way. The assets in the scheme are invested in accordance with the objectives which are laid out in the legal document which governs the scheme and which investors can study to establish whether the scheme meets their own requirements. These schemes permit investors to invest in a spread of investments in a way that would not be possible if they had to buy shares in each of the underlying companies.

3.1 Diversification through Collective Investments

Learning Objective 4.3.1

Collective investment schemes such as unit trusts enable investors to spread small sums of money across a range of financial assets in a range of different markets. The benefits of this level of diversification would not otherwise be available to them

Collective investment schemes have a vast array of different objectives. These range from general funds, investing worldwide with the objective of providing capital growth and/or income, to highly specialised schemes concentrating on a very narrow marketplace, such as a single country or a single industry, and everything in between. Exchange-traded funds offer schemes that invest in commodities such as gold or oil, without having to store bars of gold beneath the bed or barrels of oil in the garage.

Collective investment schemes permit a degree of diversification that would otherwise be impossible for the ordinary investor and difficult even for a millionaire! They offer a spread of investment while permitting interests in overseas countries or areas of the world without suffering the costs of owning overseas shares and still enjoying the protection offered by the UK regulatory oversight.

3.2 Economies of Scale

Learning Objective 4.3.2

Buying in bulk is usually cheaper than buying in small amounts. Collective investment schemes enable small investors to take advantage of these 'purchasing economies of scale'

Schemes permit investors to invest very modest amounts without the cost of doing so taking a disproportionate share of their savings. Some schemes permit investments as small as £5 a month, whereas the minimum cost effective investment in the shares of an individual company is around £3,000. Investors also enjoy a much larger degree of regulatory protection. By law, the assets of the scheme are ring-fenced and held by a trustee, generally a major international bank completely separate from the manager of the scheme.

3.3 Professional Management

Learning Objective 4.3.3

By clubbing together in a collective investment scheme, small investors can afford to pay for expert financial advice

Investors in schemes also enjoy the benefits of professional management of the assets that normally they would only enjoy if they had a substantial portfolio large enough to interest an investment manager. If they are interested in investing in a foreign country, they can use a scheme where the management is actually resident in that country, close to the market and all the local news and in the same time zone.

4. Syndication

Learning Objective 4.4

Risk can be spread through syndication

Learning Objective 4.4.1

Banks and other lenders can spread their risk on very large loans by setting up a syndicate and parcelling up the loan among the syndicate members

A company or government wishing to raise a substantial amount of money through a loan typically only want to talk to a very limited number of banks or other financial institutions, saving effort as well as restricting the discussions to those institutions with which a relationship has already been established. However, these banks might be reluctant to lend the amount of money required, as this would impose too large a concentration of risk on their own balance sheet. They therefore syndicate the loans. The lead managers amongst the banks offer other banks a share of the loan and these banks in turn will offer a share to other banks.

For instance, say a group of banks arranges a loan to the UK government on a syndicated basis. These lead banks will ask a bank in each of the continents to be a second level manager and the second level managers will in turn ask a bank in each country in their area to act as the third level manager and spread the loan amongst banks in their country. The fees are agreed with the government for the arrangement of the loan and are spread through all the banks in accordance with their position in the pecking order. It follows that a lead bank in this facility may find itself in the third or fourth level of a loan to another country, organised by a different group of banks.

4.1 Securitisation

The section above described what happens when a single loan potentially takes up too large a proportion of the bank's balance sheet. Banks can also find that though they were successfully marketing loans to the retail market they have to stop because the regulations will not allow them to make any further loans of that type. The bank might then choose to securitise a bundle of the loans and offer them to investors in the form of bonds – effectively selling the loans. Good quality bundles are attractive to investing institutions such as pension funds as they are long-dated income-producing bonds that match their pension liabilities.

Properly done, with good quality assets, such as mortgages to good quality borrowers, this benefits both the bank, which can continue to lend, and the investors who have a stream of returns that they can rely on. Unfortunately, in the years leading up to the 2007 financial crash, too many of these bundles consisted of loans to 'NINJA' (no income, no jobs or assets) borrowers, largely in the US, and the concept became tarnished. Even when the securitised bundles contained quality assets, it was feared that they did not and were therefore difficult or even impossible to sell. However, securitisation is likely to return in due course as it is too useful a concept when properly managed to ignore.

4.2 Insurance Syndication and Reinsurance

Learning Objective 4.4.2

Insurers can spread their risk by insuring jointly with other insurance companies working as a syndicate, or they can insure themselves with other insurance companies (this is known as reinsurance)

In the way we saw with banks, the same process occurs with insurance companies. When insurance companies insure a risk that is too large for their balance sheet, for instance a North Sea oil rig or a nuclear power station, they will look to pass on part of the risk to other insurance companies. This type of syndication is generally called reinsurance. As well as passing on part of the risk to their colleagues and competitors in the industry, they will also use specialist reinsurance companies. These companies do not market or take on risk from the general public but will only look for business from the large insurance companies who wish to spread the risk on their books. A number of these reinsurance companies are based in Lloyds of London, another of the international markets based in the City of London.

🗎 Chapter Questions

Based on what you have learned in Chapter Four, try to answer the following questions.

Think of an answer for each question and refer to the appropriate section for confirmation.

1. Explain how insurance relies on mutual interest.

    Answer reference: Section 1.1

    ....

    ....

2. What are the two main ways that an insurance company makes a profit out of insurance?

    Answer reference: Sections 1.3 and 1.4

    ....

3. How does diversification reduce risk?

    Answer reference: Section 2

    ....

    ....

4. Describe how a collective investment fund works.

    Answer reference: Section 3

    ....

5. What are the similarities and differences between syndication and reinsurance?

    Answer reference: Section 4

    ....

    ....

Competing for our Money

5

1. Introduction   57

2. Calculating the Return on an Investment   58

3. Valuing Shares   60

This syllabus area will provide approximately 2 of the 30 examination questions

Competing for our Money

1. Introduction

Learning Objective 5

Banks and building societies compete with each other to attract savers' deposits. Companies compete to attract investors' money – either in the form of shares (equities) or loans (bonds)

When it comes to savings, deposit takers, such as banks and building societies, and the stock market compete to attract investors' money. The deposit takers need deposits that they can subsequently lend out to grow their the business. The more cheaply and easily they can raise deposits, the more profitably they can lend.

It may be more difficult to understand why companies are keen to have a rising share price. In fact, the success of a company is often judged by the success of its shares. That success, in turn, encourages the company's customers to do business with it. Moreover, companies are happy to reward successful managers and staff with shares, giving employees at all levels a stake in the company. A rising share price can therefore improve employees' wealth which, in turn, improves their morale, making them work harder, which increases the company's profits and therefore the company's share price and so the virtuous circle continues.

After a financial adviser has drawn up an overall policy as to what type of investments to buy, in line with the investor's risk profile, policy and long-term aims, the investor has to be decide which individual stock or security to buy/invest in by comparing the overall return of the various possibilities on offer. The return is made up of income and/or capital growth.

2. Calculating the Return on an Investment

Learning Objective 5.1

Investors choose where to invest their money on the basis of projected total return over the life of the investment. Total return is the combination of income and capital gain arising from that investment

Learning Objective 5.1.2

The difference between the purchase price of an investment (such as a property, share or bond) and its current market price is called a capital gain (or loss, as the case may be). It is usually expressed as a percentage of the original purchase price. This gain (or loss) is only realised if the investment is actually sold

Learning Objective 5.1.3

To calculate total return, divide the selling price of the investment plus any dividends/interest received, by its total cost

The total return includes income, which often arrives regularly over the life of the investment, and the capital gain, which will only be guaranteed when the investment is sold, if there is one. All the income received and the difference between the cost and the proceeds are added together to make the total return. To turn this into a percentage so it can be compared with other opportunities on a level basis, the return is divided by the original

investment and multiplied by 100. This will give the percentage return. For instance:

Original investment	£1,000
Total income received	£200
Proceeds at sale	£1,500

Total Return =

$$\frac{\text{proceeds at sale + total income received - original investment}}{}$$

£1,500 + £200 - £1,000 = £700

Percentage   700/1,000 x 100 = 70%

Dividing the total return by the number of years the investment has been held will give a simple annualised return which can be used to compare with other possible investments.

2.1 Yield

Learning Objective 5.1.1

Yield is the income from an investment expressed as a percentage of the initial outlay for that investment. Examples: interest as a percentage of a savings deposit or dividend as a percentage of a share's purchase price, or interest as a percentage of a bond's purchase price

If an investment pays an income, this can be calculated as a percentage, known as yield, to compare with other investments or deposits. This is calculated as:

(Income received in one year/value) x 100

It can be calculated using the total income received from the holding divided by the value of the whole or by using the income received from one unit, for instance one share, divided by the value of that unit. As an example, let us assume a holding of 1,000 shares worth £3,000 and giving an income of £75 a year since each share receives a dividend of 7.5p. The income on each share is 7.5p and the price of each share is £3 or 300p.

The yield on this can be calculated in two ways:

Total holding	75/3000 x 100 = 2.5%
Unit	7.5/300 x 100 = 2.5%

A change in the value of a unit, and therefore of the total holding, will change the yield. If the price of the share quoted above falls to £2.50, the yield will rise to 3% (7.5/250 x 100). However, if the price increases to £3.50, the yield will fall to 2.14% (7.5/350 x 100).

2.2 Comparing Yields

Learning Objective 5.2.2
Yield advantage is the extent by which the yield on one investment exceeds the yield on another investment with a similar risk profile

Learning Objective 5.2.3
If a rival investment starts offering a higher yield, to stay competitive, other investments must either increase their yield too. If they do not, investors will switch to the higher-yielding investment

Learning Objective 5.3
If the income stream (eg, interest or dividend) from an investment cannot be increased, the only way to increase the yield is for the price to fall (because yield = income/price x 100). When price goes down, yield goes up, and vice versa

Most yield calculations are made on the basis of the total income received during the year divided by the value, for the sake of simplicity. However, where compound interest works its magic, the frequency with which payments are made can alter the actual yield calculation. For example, take two deposits both with the same headline interest offer of say 3%, but with one the income is paid only at the end of the year,

while the other pays income monthly. The actual yield of the second account is 3.04%. This may not seem a great deal of difference but if we are looking at two banks offering the different services, each with, say, £10 billion deposited by customers, the second bank will be paying £4 million more interest than the first.

The other parameter to be considered when deciding where savings are to be deposited is risk, and particularly the risk of loss. In the UK, bank deposits are explicitly guaranteed by the banking industry up to £85,000 and there is also an understanding that the government will step in and guarantee deposits for ordinary investors, as happened in the 2007 financial crash. However, it is possible to deposit money with other institutions, which pay a higher rate of interest, but which do not enjoy a banking guarantee. The higher risk may be reflected in the higher interest rate on offer but the investor has to judge whether it is a sufficient difference to justify the extra risk.

2.3 Bond Prices and Yields

Learning Objective 5.3.2
If interest rates rise, bond prices will fall because bonds pay a fixed rate of interest

Learning Objective 5.2.1
Investors will require a higher yield in return for taking on a higher risk. Investors in shares, for instance, will require a higher yield than they would on cash deposits at a bank

Most bonds offer a fixed rate of interest and that rate of interest reflects the market rate at the time the bond was issued for sale. When interest rates change, so do the prices of bonds so that the yield at the time reflects the yields generally available elsewhere in the market. The price also reflects the risk that the bond may not be repaid and that the issuer may cease to pay the promised interest. Bonds issued by the British government are generally regarded as the safest and are known as gilts because the original certificates were gilt edged. The name also reflected the quality of the bond as an investment.

Figure 6 displays the history of the Bank of England base rate since the end of the Second World War. Base rate is the interest rate at which the Bank of England will lend to other banks that have a need for liquidity. Interest rates for gilts have generally been above that level by at least 1% and the rates for other bonds have been higher, depending upon the risk.

The prices of bonds have moved in line with interest rates. For instance, the price of 3.5% War Loan fell from around £101 in 1950 to £18 in 1980 and currently stands (May 2014) at around £85. You can see from Figure 6 that the high price occurred when interest rates were low and that the low price reflected the very high interest rates at the time. Since the amount of income obtainable from a given amount of a bond remains constant, the price will reflect how valuable that income is to a purchaser and whether a better bargain is available elsewhere.

2.4 Yields

Learning Objective 5.2

If the intention is to hold onto an investment for the income and not to realise any capital gain by selling it, the yield alone must compare favourably with those of other competing investments

---

Where all things are equal and income is the investment objective, yield alone decides which investment to purchase. In practice, all things are never equal and there are always differences in term, risk, or potential for growth that makes the investment advisor's life more difficult and ensures that providing the answer to the question 'what shall I invest in?' is never easy. It may be that the yield of an investment compares favourably with its competitors because the risk is higher or the investor needs to tie up his money for longer or that other investment are likely to produce a higher return in the longer term. For instance, an annuity (see Chapter 9, Section 4.1) will probably produce the highest yield but the investor will not get any of his investment back.

3. Valuing Shares

Comparing deposit accounts and bonds is fairly simple since all the income is typically paid out. A company, however, does not have to pay out all of the profits in dividends and can sometimes pay out more than the profits. As a result, it is necessary to value shares in various different ways.

3.1 Dividend Yield

One way of assessing the value of a share is to look at its dividend yield. Shares receive income in the form of dividends and these can be paid out annually, half yearly or quarterly. Calculating the yield was shown in Section 2 of this chapter. However, the yield figure quoted against the share prices of companies in newspapers, such as the *Financial Times* and the *Daily Telegraph*, cannot be directly compared with the rates quoted for bonds or deposit accounts. The latter are quoted gross without taking income tax into account, while share yields are quoted assuming that basic rate income tax has been paid (since this is tax, it is actually more complicated than that but the above describes the effect on most peoples' tax bill).

Since shares are considered riskier than bonds and deposit accounts, the average yield on shares is usually higher than that of bonds. It is stock market opinion that when the yield on shares falls below the yield on bonds, stock market prices are too high and are likely to fall at some point in the not too distant future.

Bank Base Rate

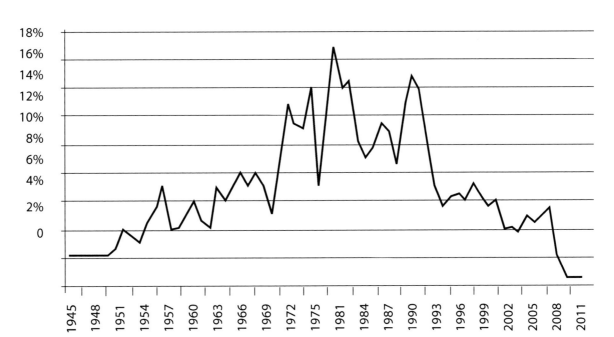

Source: ONS - Bank of England

Figure 6

However, it is equally possible that the position may be corrected by interest rates rising and bond prices falling.

3.2 Price Earnings Ratios

Most companies only pay out a proportion of their profits as dividends. Some companies pay no dividends, either because they have not made a profit or because they wish to keep the funds to ensure faster growth for the company. This is particularly so with some of the 'dot com' companies. It is therefore necessary to have a different method of measuring companies in order that they can be compared with each other. The usual way, which is found in the financial pages of newspapers, is to calculate the price earnings ratio.

The price in this calculation is the price of the shares as quoted on the stock exchange. The price can change from second to second and this will change the price earnings ratio. The earnings figure is the net profit after tax that the company makes in the year divided by the

number of shares the company has issued. For example:

Company's profit after tax	£1,000,000
Number of shares issued	10,000,000
Earnings per share	10p

If the share price is £1.30, then the price earnings ratio is 13 (£1.30/10p).

A high price earnings ratio generally means that the market thinks that the company will increase profits dramatically in the future, making the shares rise more than a company with a low price earnings ratio. Sometimes, however, it will mean that the company is barely profitable and the high price earnings ratio is purely the mathematical result of dividing a low share price by a tiny earnings figure. Investors treat the price to earnings ratio as the starting point for further research before investing in a company.

3.3 Interest/Rent Correlation

Learning Objective 5.3.1

If interest rates rise, investors in buy-to-let flats will demand higher rents to restore the yield advantage of their investment

When property is considered an investment and not just a roof over the buyer's head, it will be valued in comparison with other investment possibilities and particularly with the interest obtainable from deposits or bonds. This particularly refers to buy-to-let property investment which is sensitive to movements in interest rates. Not only does investment in property compete with deposits but much of it also is financed with borrowed money. The effect of this is known as 'gearing' and was covered in Section 2.2 in Chapter 3.

If interest rates rise, the margin between the income (rent) on the property and interest on deposits is reduced and the cost of servicing the mortgage to buy the property is increased. The landlord will therefore look to increase the rent to offset this reduction in profitability. A fall in interest rates will, of course, increase the profitability of the investment for the landlord, but most landlords will consider this to be a windfall and are most unlikely to offer a rent reduction.

Buy-to-let properties are involved in two separate but connected markets. The question of whether to buy a property to rent out is heavily influenced by the availability of other possible investments, such as bonds, and the question as to which is likely to be the most profitable investment. Prospective tenants are supremely uninterested in the outlook for bonds and deposit accounts, being only (and sensibly) interested in whether a particular property will suit their requirements at the right price for their budget.

If an increase in house prices is not expected and the property is regarded purely from the point of view of the income it produces, the landlord will look to charge a rate that is higher than the interest rate obtainable on a deposit, if only to offset the extra costs of owning a property, such as rates and repairs. However, the rate will be dictated more by the supply and demand of tenants, than by the movement of interest rates which will mainly affect the original decision on whether to buy, rather than ongoing rental prices.

Chapter Questions

Based on what you have learned in Chapter Five, try to answer the following questions.

Think of an answer for each question and refer to the appropriate section for confirmation.

1. The yield and value of various investments are given below. What is the income on each one?

    £3,600 with a yield of 4.2%
    £8,335 with a yield of 7.6%
    £7,749 with a yield of 2.6%

    Answer reference: Section 2.1

    ....

    ....

2. Where two investments have the same quoted interest rate, but the first pays interest annually and the second pays quarterly, which will have the higher AER?

    Answer reference: Section 2.2

    ....

3. Why is the dividend yield of a share not a sufficient valuation tool?

    Answer reference: Section 3.1

    ....

    ....

4. Is a share with a high price earnings ratio more likely to be high growth or low growth?

    Answer reference: Section 3.2

    ....

    ....

5. Why can a rising share price be good for a company?

    Answer reference: Section 3.2

    ....

    ....

6

The Role of Governments in an Economy

1. The Role of Governments in an Economy   67

2. Fiscal Policy   70

3. Borrowing   71

4. The Role of the Financial Regulators   72

This syllabus area will provide approximately 3 of the 30 examination questions

The Role of Governments in an Economy

1. The Role of Governments

Learning Objective 6

Central banks act on behalf of their governments in setting interest rates for an economy. Governments also intervene in the economy directly through the setting of taxes, the spending of tax revenue on public services and by the creation of laws that govern the way people do business

In the 18th century, the role of the government was largely confined to the maintenance of national security and law and order. This role has expanded immensely until there are very few aspects of life that are not influenced or controlled by the government. As an example, in 1730 there were around 11 staff in the Home Office but in 2011–12 there were 32,712. This chapter concentrates on the role of the Government and its agencies in business and finance.

The government is responsible for the legislation and regulation that govern financial services. Either directly or through the central bank, it is responsible for monetary policy such as setting interest rates, thus influencing expenditure by both consumers and business. Since the government is also responsible for raising money through taxes, it can use tax as a means of influencing business and saving.

1.1 Monetary Policy

Learning Objective 6.1

Central banks, such as the Bank of England, set the rate of interest at which they will lend to the banking system. These form the 'base' rate from which all other interest rates are derived

In the UK, the central bank, the Bank of England, is responsible for setting interest rates. However, the government is responsible for setting the targets the bank should aim for and therefore strongly influences interest rate policy. The Bank of England sets base rate, which is the rate at which it will lend to the banking system to ensure liquidity. All other interest rates are based on the base rate in theory but the Bank of England can take other steps to ensure that its policy is followed by the banking industry.

Following the 2007 financial crash, the Bank of England, like many other central banks including the Federal Reserve in the United States, reduced interest rates to their lowest level certainly since the Bank was founded in 1692 and possibly ever. In order to make sure that the interest rate was kept low to prevent bankruptcies, it carried out a policy known as **quantitative easing** (QE) whereby it created money and the law of supply and demand did the rest. Ample supply and restricted demand meant that interest rates in general were kept low in line with the base rate.

In order to encourage the construction industry, the government wanted funds to be made available to banks and building societies to lend to house buyers at very low rates to encourage them to buy houses. The government also encouraged banks to lend to industry to encourage investment. The Bank of England used its powers in the market to fulfil the government's policy.

The situation in Europe is slightly different because the currency is the euro and it has been adopted by a number of countries. The European Central Bank (ECB) is responsible for setting interest rates but it is technically independent of any of the governments of the countries where the euro is the currency. It is, however, heavily influenced by the German government and the German central bank, the Bundesbank, as Germany has by far the largest economy. Interest rates therefore tend to be set to meet German requirements, which are, in turn, heavily influenced by German memories of the hyperinflation of the 1920s, and this has caused problems in other countries, particularly in southern Europe.

1.1.1 The Use of Interest Rates to Influence Expenditure

Learning Objective 6.1.1

With so much consumer spending relying on borrowed money, the more expensive money is to borrow, the less spending there will be in an economy – and vice versa

The current level of household debt in the UK is around £1.4 trillion, much of it mortgage related but a significant amount is related to general expenditure. Figure 7 illustrates this.

It follows that a change in the interest rate can have a significant effect on the amount of money available for consumer expenditure. A rise will divert money from general expenditure to interest while a fall will have the opposite effect. An interest movement also has an effect on sentiment – on how well off consumers feel and on how prepared they are to spend.

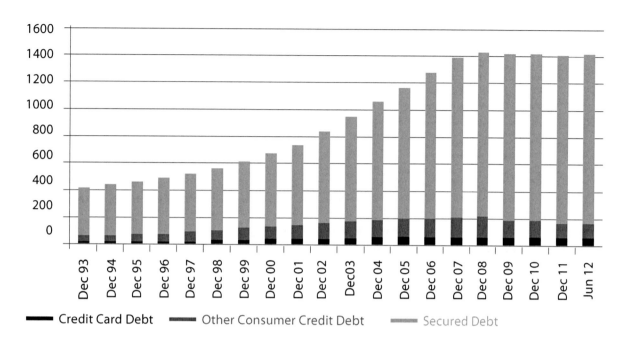

Total UK Personal Debt (£ Billions)

Source: Credit Action's September 2012 report based on Bank of England data

Figure 7

Governments can therefore use interest rates as a tool with which to nudge the economy. However, this tool has to be used very carefully as an over-enthusiastic interest rate move can spook the markets, destroying sentiment. Even an indication that the authorities are thinking of making a change to the interest rate can be enough to alter the direction of the stock market.

1.2 Saving and Interest Rates

Learning Objective 6.1.2

Higher interest rates make savings accounts more attractive as an investment, which makes other investments such as equities and bonds appear less attractive

Interest is the reward for saving. The higher the interest rate, the more attractive it may seem to save money on deposit. This may be at the expense of investing in equities and

bonds. A high interest rate will tend to deter companies from investing and reduce profits because of the increased cost of borrowing. Equally, rising interest rates will have the effect of depressing bond prices, making them less attractive too. However, the reason for raising interest rates may be because inflation has grown too high. Even with high interest rates, if inflation is at a still higher rate, the real interest rate will be negative and the investor may be losing more value through inflation than he is gaining through a high interest rate.

2. Fiscal Policy

Learning Objective 6.2

Governments impose taxes on income and spending to fund spending on public services such as health and education. Governments also borrow money from investors when tax revenue is insufficient to cover their planned expenditure

Governments need to raise money in order to pay for the expenses of government, social benefits, health, education and national security, which also covers the armed forces. Tax has always been part of life and while no taxpayer likes paying tax, they can become habitualised to it. Income tax was first introduced in 1798 as a temporary measure. It is most unlikely that the UK government will ever abolish it. The art of taxation was laid down by the Roman Emperor Tiberius in around 15 AD, who described it as being like plucking geese, where the skill was to pluck the maximum number of feathers with the minimum amount of hissing.

Governments design taxes and decide on tax rates both to raise money and to fulfil policy ambitions. The ideal tax will do both. They use tax to nudge consumers and companies to undertake activity that the government wants them to. For instance, inheritance tax was designed, particularly by socialist governments, to break the power of the great landed estates and spread wealth. By and large, they succeeded in the first policy but failed in the second in that the money merely became part of government expenditure.

There is a careful balance between the maximum amount of tax the government can raise without depressing economic activity and the amount it wishes to spend. If the two do not match, there is an imbalance. If the government spends less than it raises in tax, it can use the excess to pay off previous debt. If it raises too little to cover its expenditure, it needs to borrow to cover the difference. That difference may arise because of a fall in economic activity in the country, such as happened after the 2007 financial crash, reduced tax revenues or

because the government wishes to invest in assets which it considers will produce a return in future years that will pay off the borrowing.

2.1 Taxation

Learning Objective 6.2.1

Governments impose taxes directly, through income and corporation tax; and indirectly through VAT

Taxes are described as being either direct or indirect. Direct taxes are those paid directly by the person being charged the tax and also considered to be those taxes which cannot be moved to other people. Income tax, wealth tax, such as inheritance tax, and council tax are all direct taxes.

Indirect taxes are generally those that are charged as part of a transaction, with value added tax (VAT) being the most noted. However, stamp duty on the purchase of shares and property, excise duty on alcohol and tobacco and fuel tax are all indirect taxes. Although, like all taxes, they are eventually paid by individual taxpayers, they are actually paid to the government by the company that is selling the goods being taxed to the individual. The company, of course, recoups the tax by increasing the charge to the eventual purchaser.

2.2 "Leaning Against The Wind"

Learning Objective 6.2.2

Governments will often spend more when the economy is growing too slowly and cut back on spending when the economy is growing too fast

The great economist, John Maynard Keynes, recommended that governments should use their taxing and spending powers to even out economic activity during booms and depressions. When the economy is expanding, the government should raise more tax than it spends, paying off debt, but also acting as a brake to prevent inflation and the economy

Public Net Debt
United Kingdom from 1900 to 2015

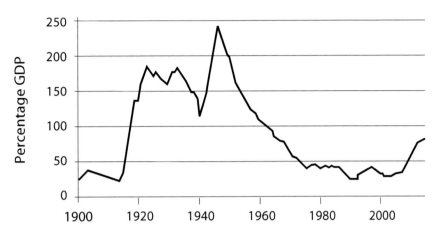

Source: UKpublicspending.com

Figure 8

from overheating. On the other hand, when the economy is declining and moving into a depression, the government should increase spending to reduce the impact on voters. This is known as 'leaning against the wind' and was first laid down by Joseph of the 'coat of many colours' fame. When First Minister in Egypt some 3,000 years ago, he saved in the seven fat years to ensure that there was no starvation in the seven lean years that followed.

There is always a temptation for governments to spend more. Voters expect it and there is always the hope that future growth will cover the extra expenditure. This is, however, like keeping the foot on the accelerator when going downhill and can lead to the danger of a financial crash, as happened in 2007.

3. Borrowing

Learning Objective 6.3

Governments borrow mainly through the issuance of bonds. In the UK, government bonds are called gilts and account for a large proportion of the bond market

As explained above, governments are regular borrowers, largely in the bond market. UK government bonds are called gilts and these

usually enjoy an AAA rating as one of the most secure debt issuers. Even when they are repaying debt because the economy is doing well, they will still need to borrow to replace old debt that is due for repayment. Since many investors, but particularly pension funds, rely on government securities to provide the flow of funds that allows them to pay pensions, there is always a ready market for bond issues.

Figure 8 illustrates British government debt since 1900 compared to gross domestic product (GDP) or the size of the British economy. You can see that the two world wars could only be fought and won because Britain was able to increase its debt massively, both in absolute terms and as a proportion of GDP. The decline shown on the chart since 1950 is not so much a decline in total nominal amount borrowed but reflects the increase of the economy since that time.

3.1 Fiscal Deficits

Learning Objective 6.3.1

When governments try to counteract the effects of economic recession, they often spend more than their revenue

Fiscal deficits occur when governments spend more than their revenue. The biggest producer of fiscal deficits is war, as is illustrated in Figure 8. However, governments also borrow when they are trying to counteract the effects of economic recession and also when they are investing in the hope of boosting growth in the future. The success of the German economy since the Second World War can be largely ascribed to the fact that it borrowed heavily, largely from the US, to replace the industry destroyed during the war. Britain, on the other hand, borrowed similar amounts but invested it in housing and the NHS.

Another source of fiscal deficits is political economic mismanagement. For instance, Argentina has turned from the sixth richest country in the world to the 26th (in 2012 according to the UN), largely through mismanagement and the policies its politicians have pursued. More recently Greece has suffered due to the various governments overspending to buy votes and having austerity imposed upon it thereby reducing the value of loans to the country significantly.

3.2 Government Debt

Learning Objective 6.3.2

Fiscal deficits can build up year after year, until countries are so overwhelmed by debt that investors are unwilling to lend them any more

A continuing series of fiscal deficits can build up to such an extent that they will eventually overcome the country's ability to repay the debt or even to pay the interest due. Many in the financial markets are of the opinion that the tipping point at which it becomes difficult for a country to recover is when debt is equal to 100% of GDP. This is, of course, a rough rule of thumb and depends upon each country looked at individually. However, when a country approaches that kind of level, it can find it impossible to borrow more. The financial markets see no point in throwing good money after bad.

At that point, there are a number of options for the indebted country. There are multinational agencies, such as the International Monetary Fund (IMF), which will lend funds. However, these loans are subject to strict conditions, designed to bring the country back to economic viability and also to ensure that the lenders get their money back. The result is generally unpleasant for the ordinary citizens of the country as it involves cuts in salaries and benefits to help balance the books.

If the country's leaders are unable to sell the IMF remedy to their people, and the market is not prepared to lend any more, the only alternative is to default on the country's debt. This usually results in the exclusion of the country from the money markets for a number of years until the country's economy has recovered sufficiently for lenders to trust it again. In view of the penalties involved, default is usually only undertaken as a last resort.

4. The Role of the Financial Regulators

Learning Objective 6.4

Economies require a stable and well-functioning financial system. Governments appoint regulators to ensure that banks and other financial service providers follow laws and treat their customers fairly

Now that the money in your pocket and in your bank account is largely reflected by computer blips and not a pile of gold, a reputation for being safe, honest and fair is the basis for a successful, long-lasting financial business. This, in turn, relies on good regulation to ensure that members of the industry follow the rules and that customers are safeguarded.

In the UK, responsibility for compliance with the rules for the financial services industry is in the hands of two institutions, the Bank of England and the Financial Conduct Authority (FCA). Many of the rules emanate from the European Union though the UK is heavily involved in designing the rules before they come into power.

4.1 The Bank of England

Learning Objective 6.4.1

The Bank of England sets interest rates through its Monetary Policy Committee; it regulates banks and other financial firms through the Prudential Regulation Authority

---

As well as controlling monetary policy through interest rates, the Bank is also responsible for ensuring the good financial health of the UK banking and financial services industries. Its subsidiary, the Prudential Regulation Authority (PRA), is responsible for ensuring the prudential management of banks and other financial firms through regulation and audit. It makes sure that firms retain adequate reserves to meet their liabilities and that they are managed in such a way as not to pose a risk to the UK economy.

4.2 The Financial Conduct Authority (FCA)

Learning Objective 6.4.2

The Financial Conduct Authority regulates the way financial services firms deal with their customers and with each other

---

The FCA is responsible for regulating the relationship between financial firms and their customers and between each other. Communications issued by financial firms must be fair, clear and not misleading. The FCA ensures the safety of client assets by issuing rules under which the assets are held and regularly auditing the position, and also regulates how firms should conduct themselves with each other and with their customers

and when firms must communicate with their customers.

Most of the rules promulgated by the UK regulators emanate from the EU and are based on EU directives. The objective of the directives is to ensure a level playing field in Europe and facilitate cross-border sales. Since the UK has the largest and most sophisticated financial services sector, it should benefit handsomely from this.

📑 Chapter Questions

Based on what you have learned in Chapter Six, try to answer the following questions.

Think of an answer for each question and refer to the appropriate section for confirmation.

1. How does the UK government influence the Bank of England over the setting of interest rates?

    Answer reference: Section 1.1

    ....

    ....

2. How can governments use interest rates to influence expenditure?

    Answer reference: Section 1.1.1

    ....

    ....

3. How can governments use tax to influence behaviour?

    Answer reference: Section 2

    ....

    ....

4. What options do governments have if they can no longer meet their debt obligations?

    Answer reference: Section 3.2

    ....

    ....

5. What are the responsibilities of the regulatory institutions in the UK financial services industry?

    Answer reference: Section 4

    ....

7

The Role of the Private Sector in an Economy

1. Introduction   77

2. Factors of Production   78

3. Factor Incomes   79

4. Profit Maximisation   80

This syllabus area will provide approximately 2 of the 30 examination questions

The Role of the Private Sector in an Economy

1.   Introduction

Learning Objective 7

In Europe, governments account for about 40-60% of economic activity, depending on the individual country. The remainder is undertaken by the private sector, operating in markets where the interaction between households and firms establishes the supply and demand for goods and services

The economy can be divided into two parts. The public sector consists of that part managed by the government and paid for by taxation. The private sector covers the rest of the economy and is responsible for producing the tax revenues that pay for the public sector.

Depending on which country is being looked at, the proportion of the public sector varies between 40% and 60% in Europe, with the UK having a public sector that accounts for around 45% of the economy. Economists generally consider that a public sector of no more than 35% of GDP or the total turnover of the country is what countries should aim for and the UK achieved this in the years leading up to the end of the last millennium.

The extra expenditure undertaken by the UK government at the beginning of the current century and the 2007 financial crash has meant that the public sector now makes up a much larger proportion of the economy in order to mitigate the effects of the crash. It must be remembered, however, that a vibrant private sector is the best source of growth in new jobs and, as such, should be nurtured by the government.

1.1 Households and Firms

Learning Objective 7.1

Economists divide the private sector into households and firms. The two interact in a circular flow of buying and selling of goods and services

The private sector, in turn, is divided into two – households and firms. Households provide the workers who work in the firms and the consumers that buy the goods and services provided by the firms. This division tends to ignore the role of exports in the increasingly global village in which we live and ignores the fact that the same people live in the households and staff the firms. However, it does provides a good starting point for looking at the private sector.

1.1.1 Households

Learning Objective 7.1.1

Individuals are grouped together in households. Households wish to buy goods and services provided by firms – but only at a price they are willing to pay: this is called demand

Individuals, either singly or grouped together, make up a household. Households provide the final market for all goods produced in or imported into a country. Although it may appear that, for instance, machinery is only used by firms, the firms only use it to provide the goods for the end user, the individual or household. Without the households' desire, ability to buy and willingness to pay the price, there would be no market for the goods and services produced by firms.

It follows that individuals in households effectively pay all tax as any tax that is paid by firms is passed through to the ultimate consumer in the form of increased prices. It is only right that individuals are the ones who decide who should run the country by voting in elections.

It is households, and the individuals in households, acting as consumers who create the demand for the goods and services provided by firms and decide what price they are prepared to pay.

1.1.2 Firms

Learning Objective 7.1.2

Firms wish to sell goods and services to the households. The willingness to sell a good or service at a given price is called supply

Firms react to the demand from households by offering goods and services at a price at which they consider that they will make a profit. In order to do so, they employ the individuals in households to make the goods or provide the services or sell in the shops. The incomes received by these workers allows them to provide the demand, thus creating a virtuous circle.

2. Factors of Production

Learning Objective 7.2

There are four key inputs that go into the making of any goods or the supply of any service: land, labour, capital and enterprise

The four key inputs that go to the making of any goods or the supply of any service are: land, labour, capital and enterprise. You will note that money is not one of them, being just a means of acquiring the four or a measure of their value or an intermediary in their exchange. These four are known as the factors of production and it is possible to debate as to which factor the various sub-inputs are allocated.

2.1   Land

Learning Objective 7.2.1

The term land is used to cover all the physical resources needed, such as: fields required for agriculture; the factory used for manufacturing; the shop used for a retail business; the office used by a service company

Land also covers the natural resources that are obtained from land, such as oil, timber and steel. These can be renewable, such as timber, or non-renewable, such as oil. It covers all the physical input required to make goods.

2.2   Labour

Learning Objective 7.2.2

Labour is the workforce: skilled, unskilled or a mix of both. Labour is supplied by households.

This can be extended to what is called human capital which includes all the skills and experience required in this increasingly technical age to work the machines and provide the services. Marxist economists consider Labour to be the most important of the factors, since without labour none of the goods will be produced. Labour is also responsible for the production of non physical goods, or service such as waiting at tables or teaching at a school.

2.3 Capital

Learning Objective 7.2.3

Capital is the plant and equipment used to produce goods or services. Examples of capital goods range from welding robots on a car production line to ATM machines used by banks to dispense cash to their customers

Some economists will consider buildings such as factories to be capital rather than land. Capital covers the things that labour uses to produce the goods. Even when the good is not physical, such as teachers providing an education for pupils, they will use capital such as classrooms and whiteboards.

2.4   Enterprise

Learning Objective 7.2.4

Enterprise is sometimes also known as entrepreneurship. It is the know-how or ability to combine the three other factors in order to make a good or provide a service.

Enterprise covers the bright idea which produces the goods by combining some or all of the other factors to provide goods. The 'bright idea' may be like that of a Steve Jobs in designing and iPod or a James Dyson in producing a new type of vacuum cleaner or it may be the ability to make an institution run well, such as the head of a school.

3.   Factor Incomes

Learning Objective 7.3

Each factor of production earns income in a different way

Land, labour, capital and enterprise all earn income in different ways.

3.1 Land

Learning Objective 7.3.1
Land earns rent

Land earns rent. In economic terms, this is not just the charge that must be paid to the landlord. It can also be the notional figure that, for instance, a freehold factory earns as the place that manufacturing takes place in. When looking at the profitability of the enterprise, it must be asked whether that factory would earn more as an office, a block of flats or a field for grazing sheep.

3.2 Labour

Learning Objective 7.3.2
Wages are the main way in which households earn the money they need to buy goods or services from the firms

Labour earns wages, from the newest recruit, straight from school, to the managing director. Wages are the main way in which households earn the money they need to buy goods or services from the firms.

3.3 Capital

Learning Objective 7.3.3
The money used to buy capital goods is also known as capital and is usually provided by investors or lenders. Investors and lenders seek a return on their money and they receive this in the form of dividends or interest

Capital earns interest. The money used to buy capital goods is also known as capital and is usually provided by investors or lenders. This can be done by subscribing extra money or by leaving profits in the firm (retained profits) which allow the firm to grow and make the investors' shareholding more valuable. Investors and lenders seek a return on their money and they receive this in the form of dividends, interest or retained profits which make the investment more valuable.

3.4 Enterprise

Learning Objective 7.3.4
Entrepreneurs seek a reward for their expertise, know-how and energy in the form of profits. If they do not receive their due share of the profits they generate, they will take their talents elsewhere.

Entrepreneurs seek a reward for their expertise, know-how and energy in the form of profits. If they do not receive their due share of the profits they generate, they will take their talents elsewhere.

4. Profit Maximisation

Learning Objective 7.4
Firms are presumed always to be trying to maximise their profits by buying at the lowest price and selling at the highest

Profit is sometimes considered to be something that wicked capitalists hide under their beds and spend their nights counting. In fact, we are all attempting to make a profit. For most people, profit is what they make over and above what is needed to cover their day-to-day living requirements. They will use this extra to pay for a holiday, save for a bigger pension, buy a new car or house, or buy presents for the children.

A company uses profit for two purposes. The first is to reward investors with dividends, but the second and more important is to have the extra funds to grow the firm, invest in new equipment, hire extra workers and improve the future of the firm for investors, customers and workers.

Number of units sold	Fixed costs	Variable costs	Total costs	Total Revenue	Profit/Loss
0	£1,000,000	£0	£1,000,000	£0	**−£1,000,000**
250,000	£1,000,000	£250,000	£1,250,000	£500,000	**−£750,000**
500,000	£1,000,000	£500,000	£1,500,000	£1,000,000	**−£500,000**
75,000	£1,000,000	£750,000	£1,750,000	£1,500,000	**−£250,000**
1,000,000	£1,000,000	£1,000,000	£2,000,000	£2,000,000	**£0**
1,250,000	£1,000,000	£1,250,000	£2,250,000	£2,500,000	**£250,000**
1,500,000	£1,000,000	£1,500,000	£2,500,000	£3,000,000	**£500,000**
1,750,000	£1,000,000	£1,750,000	£2,750,000	£3,500,000	**£750,000**
2,000,000	£1,000,000	£2,000,000	£3,000,000	£4,000,000	**£1,000,000**

Figure 9

Directors of firms are legally obliged to do their best to run as profitable a company as they possibly can by buying at the lowest price and selling at the highest. However, managing a firm is always a delicate balance between the long term and the short term.

Looking at the short term, a seller will always try to obtain the highest prices possible. Someone at a car boot sale attempting to sell a pile of goods he has picked up cheaply has no interest in repeat business. He is only interested in selling off the contents of his car boot and disappearing with the money, never to be seen again.

An established business is likely to operate on a longer-term basis. Its profit will come from repeat business and it is in its interests to ensure that its customers are happy with the bargain they have struck and that they will return, confident that they will be well treated, and will also tell their friends and neighbours how good the firm is. It is the strapline of the John Lewis Partnership that they are 'never knowingly undersold' and the firm goes to considerable lengths to ensure that this is accurate. If the customer finds that something he has purchased is obtainable at a lower price at another shop, John Lewis will refund the difference. As a result, the firm is considered one of the most successful retailers in the UK.

The same consideration will govern the firm's relationships with its suppliers. The firm looks for continuity of supply of quality products and this is most likely to occur in a long-term relationship where both are confident that working together will benefit both parties. One of the reasons behind this long-term view is gearing.

4.1 Gearing and Break-even

Gearing was mentioned in Section 2.2 of Chapter 3 when discussing its effect on the profit or loss made when property was acquired using borrowed money. Gearing has an effect on all companies. Before a firm manages to sell a single product, it will already have paid a whole series of costs for the factory in which the product was made: the raw materials that went into the product; the labour that made the product; and the marketing costs for selling it. Some of the costs, raw materials for instance, are only incurred if a product is made. These are known as variable costs. The other costs are the fixed costs of the operation and will be payable whether a product is made or not. These costs do not change depending on the number of products made, and a good example is rent that the firm might be paying for its property. If a firm does not make a profit or loss in a given year, it is said to be breaking even.

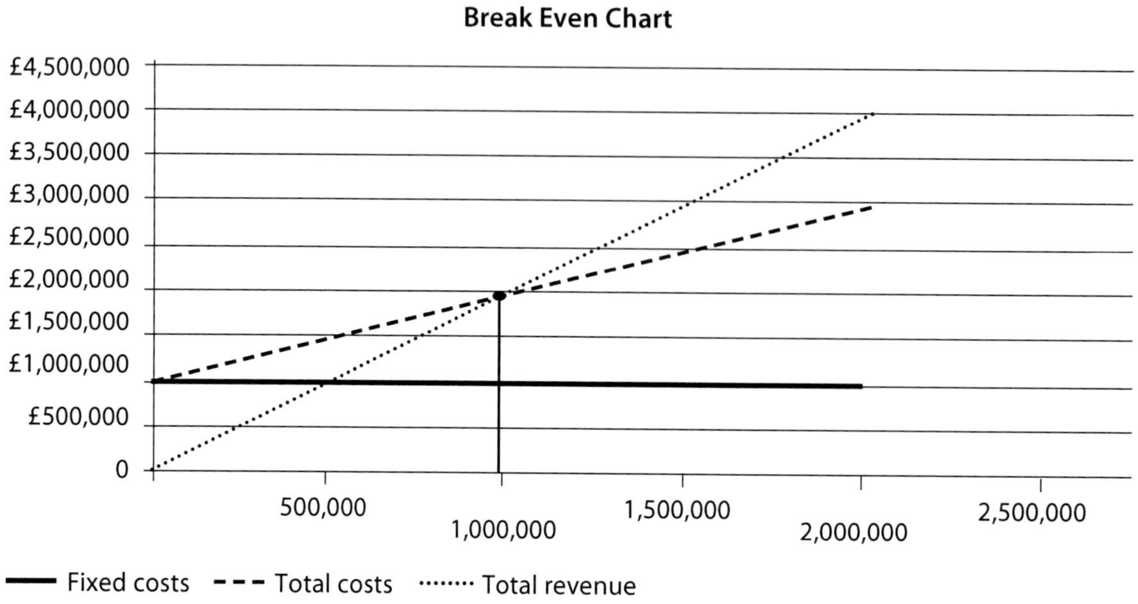

Break Even Chart

Figure 10

For example, let us assume that a factory makes widgets. The fixed costs of the factory total £1 million a year and the variable costs of each widget are £1. The firm sells the widgets at £2 each. To calculate the break-even point, the following calculation is used:

No of units sold to break-even =

$$\frac{\text{Fixed costs}}{(\text{Selling price} - \text{Variable costs per unit})}$$

In the example given above, the calculation is as follows:

No of units sold to break-even =

$$\frac{£1,000,000}{(£2-£1)}$$

No of units sold to break-even = 1,000,000 widgets

Once sales increase above one million widgets a year, the firm will start making a profit. If it manages to sell two million widgets in the year, it will have made a profit of £1 million on a turnover of £4 million. This can be seen more simply in Figure 9 and Figure 10.

In Figures 9 and 10, you can clearly see that the firm in the example needs to sell one million widgets at £2 each to break-even, which

equates to £2 million in revenue. If the firm sells any number of widgets above or below one million then the firm will make either a profit or a loss for that year. A firm can use break-even analysis to determine their strategy by modelling different levels of production and pricing to see how this will impact upon the firm's profits.

You can also see that an increase in turnover will produce a greater increase in profitability. If, in the example, the firm manages to increase turnover from £4 million to £6 million, a 50% increase, it will double profits, a 100% increase. This is the effect of gearing.

4.2   Potential for Conflict

Learning Objectives 7.4.1

The desire of firms to maximise their profits can lead them into conflict with workers, who wish to maximise their wages, and with governments, who seek the greatest output at the lowest possible cost

The desire of firms to maximise profit can bring them into conflict with the various interested parties with which they deal. Prime among these are the workers who may consider that they should benefit more from any increase in profits or just be compensated for a rise in the cost of living, whether profits are increasing or not. Again, the balance between the short term and the long term has to be considered. Many firms consider it worth paying above average wages to ensure that they have happy staff who will continue to bring their expertise and experience to benefit the firm. History has shown, however, that bad management and short-sighted, greedy, badly-lead staff have forced many companies to close. The collapse of the UK shipbuilding, aircraft manufacturing and coal mining industries over the last century can be blamed on these two factors.

Companies can also fall out with their customers, who will cease to buy the firm's products, if they consider that they are being ripped off, and with their suppliers who may cease to supply them. The result in both cases is likely to be the closure of the firm, though this may have been inevitable due to changes in market forces or poor management.

Firms can come into conflict with the government if the aims of both disagree. The government will usually win these arguments at a basic level, if only because it can rewrite the rules. However, both sides will lose if the rules fail to encourage growth and employment.

.

📃 Chapter Questions

Based on what you have learned in Chapter Seven, try to answer the following questions.

Think of an answer for each question and refer to the appropriate section for confirmation.

1. How do households and firms interact?

   Answer reference: Section 1.1

   ....
   ....

2. What are the factors of production?

   Answer reference: Section 2

   ....
   ....

3. How can 'enterprise' deserve an increased share of profits?

   Answer reference: Section 3.4

   ....
   ....

4. Should profits be entirely allocated to labour?

   Answer reference: Section 4

   ....
   ....

5. How do fixed costs impact on a firm's profitability?

   Answer reference: Section 4.1

   ....
   ....

The Function of Markets

1. The Function of Markets   87

2. Examples of Markets in Action   89

3. When Markets do not Work Properly   92

This syllabus area will provide approximately 3 of the 30 examination questions

The Function of Markets

1. The Function of Markets

Learning Objective 8

Wants are unlimited but the resources to satisfy those wants are scarce. Markets are the means by which economies find a balance between those two

The whole world is a market and everybody in it, from the youngest child buying its first packet of sweets to the oldest pensioner, affects it. The effect may be so miniscule as to be unnoticeable but there is an effect, nevertheless. The thought process of every purchaser is much the same – 'do I want to spend this amount of money on this purchase?'

That decision, multiplied by everyone who makes it, can make or ruin companies because it may mean that prospective purchasers will not touch the product with a bargepole or, alternatively, consider that it is the greatest thing since sliced bread. Markets are the means by which economies are directed to produce the goods that are wanted and to cease producing those that are no longer required. This is done through the price mechanism.

1.1 The Price Mechanism

Learning Objective 8.1

In any properly functioning market, price will establish equilibrium between the supply of goods and services and the demand for those goods and services

Theoretically, the price of something will reach equilibrium when supply equals demand and all suppliers and all purchasers consider the price ideal. In practice, this never happens except when a monopoly supplier fixes the price of something that people must have. The latter usually only happens when the state gets involved either in the supply or in fixing the price. In the real world, suppliers will always seek an advantage over their competitors while purchasers will always seek a cheaper price. A market is made up of a host of individual participants, few of whom will agree on what the price should be and their interaction will decide how a price moves. A preponderance of buyers will move the price up: more sellers will move it down, as will a lack of buyers.

1.1.1 The Market Clearing Price

Learning Objective 8.1.1

The market clearing price is the price at which suppliers are willing to sell all their goods or services and customers are willing to buy

The market clearing price is the price at which suppliers are willing to sell all their goods or services and customers are equally willing to buy them. At that point, the price should be in equilibrium. However, in practice this is never, or hardly ever, seen, or, if it is seen, it is only a very temporary phenomenon. Even if the last tin of baked beans in the supermarket is purchased at closing time, the next day will see a fresh delivery and a fresh supply of buyers.

In theory, an excess of supply over demand will see the price fall while the opposite will see the price rise. Although during a trip to the local supermarket will show price matches with those at a rival supermarket, a closer

study will reveal that many of the price cuts are actually promotional deals, largely funded by the manufacturer, whose aim is to encourage new purchasers to try the product and become regular buyers. The marketing department rather than economic theory is behind the price change. The marketing department is also behind the permanent sales that are seen in, for instance, furniture stores. Buyers are now in habit of seeing goods permanently discounted and will only buy if they feel that they are getting a good bargain.

There are also markets that do not work in line with economic theory and these are discussed below.

1.1.2 Price as a Signal

Learning Objective 8.1.2

A high price signals to producers that demand is greater than supply: they will produce more to take advantage of that high demand

Learning Objective 8.1.3

A low price signals to producers that supply is greater than demand: they will cut back production

Price, supply and demand are the three influences on the working of markets. Two of the factors will work upon the third, though which is which will change constantly. How far supply and demand will influence price depends upon the elasticity of the three factors, or, in other words, how far they can change.

It is obvious that, however great the demand, Leonardo da Vinci will never paint another picture, since he has been dead for nearly 500 years. The supply is therefore finite while demand is huge. Most people in the UK would be extremely happy to have one of his pictures on their wall if they could afford it. As a result, the price of his pictures has risen to stratospheric levels at which not even the average billionaire could afford one.

Instead of a Leonardo masterpiece, it is better to study a more ordinary item, like a tin of baked beans. Let us say that demand rises due to a fashionable doctor claiming that they will enhance longevity. The manufacturers raise the price and production becomes more profitable. Other potential manufacturers notice this and they invest in new production facilities, increasing the supply of baked beans. Farmers plant more bean plants and gradually supply becomes greater than even the enhanced demand. At this point, some manufacturers start to cut their prices to try and keep market share and production in their factories continuing. The other manufacturers follow suit and a vicious circle of falling prices and profitability occurs. Some of the manufacturers give up and close their factories and the supply becomes smaller than demand. The remaining manufacturers now find that they can raise prices and profitability increases. At this point, new manufacturers start production and the cycle continues.

The example above referred to baked beans but could have referred to any goods or services where both supply and demand can be fairly elastic. Within the cycle described, a high and rising price will indicate that demand for the product is sufficiently high for manufacturers to raise the price. In this kind of scenario, the companies have to decide on the balance between restricting supply and therefore making the product more profitable or increasing supply and selling more goods but with a lower margin of profit.

If the supply is not elastic, or, in other words, it is not possible for suppliers to produce more of the goods or services, the result of rising demand will be to increase prices until they reach such a level that demand is choked off and the price reaches equilibrium.

Equally, a low and falling price will indicate either that demand is lower than supply or that supply is much greater than demand, or, indeed, a mixture of the two. For suppliers, this scenario usually means that one or more of them will have to leave the market, cease manufacture and concentrate on something else or, at the worst, go bust.

Prices react to supply and demand most in line with the academic theory outlined above in classic marketplaces where traders concentrate

on a single type of market and the goods or services bought and sold are wholesale. Examples of these are given below in Sections 2.1 and 2.3 of where the market does not work as well as it should in Section 2.4.1 below.

2. Examples of Markets in Action

Learning Objective 8.2

Markets set the price for almost every type of human activity or need

Markets influence, and sometimes set, the price of all goods and services. They also determine their allocation across the world by setting the price of basic commodities, services and finance.

When talking about markets, most people envisage a formal market like the stock exchange. At the primary level, this is accurate but many markets are informal and spread right the way across the country or, indeed, the world. More formal markets include the commodities markets and many of the financial markets while examples of informal markets are the labour market and the property market. Formal markets are generally centralised and were often in a single building. Even in this computerised age, they are regulated and controlled, while governments take a particular interest in their doings. Government do, of course, take an interest in informal markets but these are much more difficult to regulate and practically impossible to control.

2.1   Commodity Markets

Learning Objective 8.2.1

Commodity markets set the price of essentials such as wheat, copper and oil

Commodity markets act as the intermediary between the producers of primary materials, such as metals, corn and petroleum. Many of these markets are in London, originally set up in the 18th and 19th centuries when Britain was the primary trading and manufacturing country in the world. Others were set up where they were because that was where the transport links between the producers and the consumers were. For instance, the corn and beef markets are headquartered in Chicago, where they were driven or transported from the prairies to the rail heads of the railways to the east coast cities of the US.

Forward foreign exchange was covered in Section 3.2 of Chapter 1. The same ability to sell for future delivery has long been a vital part of the commodities markets. Suppose you are a farmer and you expect a good harvest of wheat in the coming autumn. You know that you can sell this for a profit at that time but before then, you have to pay for seed, for labour and all the other expenses of growing wheat. You therefore sell your harvest now to the merchants of the commodity market, though you have not even bought the seed yet. This means that you have traded part of the profit you expect in nine months' time for the ability to buy all that is necessary now. You also have the comfort of knowing exactly how much you're getting for the ungrown wheat, no matter what the laws of supply and demand do to the price in the meantime. There are records showing that farmers were selling their harvests forward in Babylon nearly 3,000 years ago, showing how long a history commodity trading has.

2.2   Property Markets

The property market is an informal market made up of all the buyers and sellers of houses, flats, offices and land. The major difference between the property market and, for instance, the commodities markets is that property cannot be moved. Once a house has been built, it stays there until it falls down or is knocked down. Estate agents also fulfil a different role from that of the traders in one of the formal markets. Estate agents do not buy or sell houses for their own account, acting as a true intermediary, but only as an introducer between buyer and seller. Nevertheless, the price of property moves up and down in accordance with the laws of supply and demand, just like in any other market.

2.3   Financial Markets

Learning Objective 8.3

Financial markets play a key part in the pricing of interest rates for savings, loans and foreign exchange rates

Financial markets are the largest by value and by number of transactions of all the markets. The size of the foreign exchange market, at $5 trillion a day, has already been commented on in Section 3 of Chapter 1 and some of the other markets, though nowhere near the same size, still turn over trillions of dollars a year. The rates fixed on these markets form the basis for the rates charged for retail transactions on mortgages, credit cards and foreign exchange.

2.4 Money Markets

Learning Objective 8.3.1

Banks and other financial institutions lend money to each other. The interest rate they charge is often used as a benchmark, on which the interest charged on many other financial products is based

Banks and other financial institutions borrow from and lend to each other on a daily basis. It is not until the end of the working day that banks are aware of just how much money has been deposited or taken out. They therefore need to deposit excess funds, thus earning some interest, or borrow to cover any shortfall. They also borrow and deposit where they can see the possibility of making a turn, or profit, remembering what was said in Chapter 1 about the magic of big numbers. The interest charged or paid is fixed as a margin over a centrally calculated rate called the London InterBank Offered Rate, or LIBOR. LIBOR is also used as the base rate for charging long-term loans to governments and companies and it also influences mortgages and other retail loans far more than the Bank of England's base rate. Forty years ago the London money market was run by top hatted discount brokers who walked from bank head office to bank head office, finishing at the Bank of England in a way that had not changed since the 18th century. Now it is all run by computers over the internet.

2.4.1 Stock Exchanges

Learning Objective 8.3.2

Stock exchanges are markets where shares (equities) and loans (bonds) are traded. Stock exchanges match buyers and sellers automatically based on price

Stock exchanges are markets where shares and bonds are bought and sold. Market makers often act as intermediaries between buyers and sellers, moving prices in accordance with supply and demand. A market maker will offer two prices in any security, one at which he will buy (the lower price) and one at which he will sell (the higher price). He will hold shares on his own account when there is no immediate buyer available. Computerisation has allowed the stock exchange to extend trading to financial instruments derived from shares and called derivatives. These perform the same functions that forward trading does with commodities and foreign exchange, allowing investors to hedge risk (see Section 4 of Chapter 1) and also speculate without having to produce the full cost of any holding. The other effect is to gear up the profit (or loss) of any transaction.

2.4.2 Foreign Exchange Markets

Learning Objective 8.3.3

Foreign exchange transactions amount to more than US$5 trillion a day, but do not take place on formal exchanges. Buyers and sellers contact each other directly

The foreign exchange market was extensively covered in Chapter 1. Like a number of other financial markets, traders on the foreign exchange market contact each other directly or through brokers. Nowadays, most trading takes place on a computerised basis with automated systems taking the bulk of the effort. The London market is responsible for around 40% of world turnover or around $2 trillion a day.

3. When Markets do not Work Properly

Learning Objective 8.4

Sometimes markets do not function well or fail to function at all

In order to work well, markets require an agreed format underpinned by legislation that allows the rapid and confirmed transfer of ownership or the setting up of formal enforceable contracts. The UK property market is an example of a market where the legislation permits a rapid transfer of ownership which can be carried out in as little as two days, if really necessary. There are countries where transfer of land ownership takes more than a year as a minimum and involves more than 50 different government offices and still allows doubts as to the security of ownership. As a result, land ownership does not change much.

In order for markets to work well, there has to be a need for the market and, more importantly, the legislative and bureaucratic framework for speedy and secure transfer of ownership has to be in place.

3.1 Labour Markets

Learning Objective 8.2.2

Households will withdraw their labour if the wages on offer are too low and alternative, higher-paying jobs are available. During periods of high unemployment, workers' bargaining power is limited

The labour market is an informal market and involves every employee and employer in the world. It is therefore the market that touches the most people, with very few not being affected. The basic economic theory of supply and demand would indicate that where demand for workers is greater than supply, prices will rise and that they will fall when the reverse is true. A look at the employment trends since the beginning of the 21st century will show that this did not happen, particularly in the years before the 2007 crash. Although the jobs market was booming,

there was still widespread unemployment. Why? Because there was grit in the machine!

Debatably the following are all contributory factors:

- The social security benefits system, together with the high marginal tax rate for those dipping into employment meant that the benefit of getting a job was marginal at best, and, at worst, could mean that net income actually fell.
- At the beginning of the century, the then government threw open the doors to European immigrants. This relieved the pressure on curing the benefits problem. The result of the current government's reform of social security and raising of the tax allowance has improved the benefit of work for the low paid and has been rewarded by a marked increase in employment amongst the formerly long term unemployed.
- Job protection legislation and union pressure are aimed at improving and protecting the employed at the expense of the unemployed. Taking on a new member of staff who has not proved him or herself always involves the risk that an error has been made. The legislation makes it difficult to correct this.
- It can be difficult for job applicants to move to where the jobs are, due to the cost of housing, particularly in the South East.

None of these prevents the labour market from working. They just stop it working as well as it could.

3.2 Missing Markets

Learning Objective 8.4.1

Markets cannot exist where there is no practical way to charge people for using goods or services. Examples are radio programmes or street lights

There are a number of services for which no market exists. This may be because it is regarded as a social good that the state should provide and be paid for by all taxpayers. Examples of this are the UK's health service and the national road network. Another reason may be that the technology to price the service does not exist, for instance with radio programmes.

However, the fact that the technology does not exist now does not mean that it will not occur in the future. For instance, the provision of television has been revolutionised. When the BBC came into existence, it was financed by the TV licence, a tax under another name. ITV financed itself through charging for advertising. The appearance of Sky and other satellite and cable companies have changed the industry out of all recognition because the suppliers can charge individual customers for what they view.

While radio has some way to go before it charges for programmes on demand, the technology for charging for road use is already available in the form of black boxes that track cars' use of roads and the speed at which they go. The barrier to charging for road use is largely political, rather than technical, as it is for charging for the National Health Service.

3.3   Market Failure

Learning Objective 8.4.2

Sometimes markets do not allocate resources in the most efficient way. Governments will often then intervene to correct the market failure

In Section 3.2 above, there are a couple of examples of where the state runs the market. There are far more examples of where the state has intervened because it considers that the market is flawed or that it is not producing the results that the government would like. Occasionally, the government's intervention has a beneficial result but all too often it has been disastrously expensive. Some may regard the sale of council houses by the Thatcher government as having produced a home owning democracy and been beneficial. On the other hand, the policy of 'picking winners', such as the reorganisation of the UK motor car manufacturing industry in the 1960s, which resulted in the disappearance of UK owned companies, and the investment in Concorde, which was beautiful but never made a profit, can only be regarded as failures. The sale of the UK gold reserves just before the price went

up around ten times also cannot be regarded as a success.

A major problem with state intervention has been that employees of state-owned companies are also voters. There is a temptation to make decisions that are politically expedient but commercially wrong.

Where state intervention is limited to ensuring that the legislative requirements are in place and the bureaucratic framework is efficient, the state's role is highly beneficial.

3.4   Information Failure

Learning Objective 8.4.3

Sometimes people do not act in their own best interests because they lack sufficient information to make an informed decision. Young people rarely save enough for their retirement because they do not understand the cost of living for old people and the limitations of the basic state pension

All markets suffer from information failure where decisions would be very different had all the information needed been to hand. It is an old market joke that 20/20 hindsight is wonderful and that with it no mistakes would ever have been made. Even worse, the information may be available and, indeed, well known but just ignored.

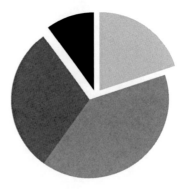

As an example, one must wonder at the lack of logic and common sense of those who decided to build the Fukushima nuclear power plant in Japan, wrecked by an earthquake and tsunami in 2011, on a well-known geological fault where earthquakes are a regular occurrence and facing an ocean prone to tsunamis. Equally, one must question the decision made in Germany to close all their nuclear power stations after the Fukushima disaster, given that Germany has never had an earthquake that has done more than rattle the teaspoons and certainly has never had a tsunami.

It is hoped that this book shows the wisdom and benefits of starting to save early for the major expenditures of life, such as house purchase, children and pensions and explains ways of doing so in a cost-effective and tax-efficient way.

📑 Chapter Questions

Based on what you have learned in Chapter Eight, try to answer the following questions.

Think of an answer for each question and refer to the appropriate section for confirmation.

1. Explain how demand influences price.

    Answer reference: Section 1.1.1

    ....

    ....

2. Explain how price influences demand.

    Answer reference: Section 1.1.1 and 1.1.2

    ....

    ....

3. What are the differences between formal and informal markets?

    Answer reference: Section 2

    ....

4. Why do markets fail to work?

    Answer reference: Section 3

    ....

    ....

5. How does state intervention help and hinder markets?

    Answer reference: Section 3.3

    ....

    ....

9

Planning for the Future

1. Introduction   99

2. Savings and Investments   100

3. Pensions   101

4. Annuities (The Pension Pot)   103

5. Wills   105

This syllabus area will provide approximately 3 of the 30 examination questions

Planning for the Future

Planning for the Future

1. Introduction

Learning Objective 9

Many people wish to buy their own home at some point in their lives, and everyone hopes to retire. These require substantial sums to be saved. The earlier people start to save, the better

Wanting to buy expensive items has always required planning and saving. This is especially so when talking about the most expensive items in life, housing, retirement and children. These also require using all the assistance available from savings institutions, the tax authorities, planning ahead and the magic of compound interest.

Even the most relaxed of mortgage lenders now requires a considerable deposit before lending. Given that the average house is now worth in the region of £300,000, even a 10% deposit is a sizeable sum. Moreover, the larger the deposit, the lower the interest rate on, and the more available, a mortgage is. Retirement can last for more than a third of a lifetime and can equal a working life. The working life therefore has to pay for not only the expenses of living during that time but also the expenses of perhaps more than 40 years after retirement. As for having children, these can be even more expensive than houses or retirement!

It is possible to live without planning or saving, relying on the state for assistance, but it is generally far more pleasant if you can afford the extras that make life worth living but these require planning and saving for.

2. Savings and Investments

Learning Objective 9.1

Financial service providers offer a number of products to help people save. These include life assurance products, individual savings accounts (ISAs)

Where there is a demand, there will be a product and financial services are no different. There is a myriad of products and services designed to help savers look after their money and guide them through the maze of possible ways to take best advantage of what is on offer. Since saving is considered to be something that should be encouraged, the state acts to assist savers in a number of ways. Apart from general encouragement, the state also ensures that most saving is protected through regulation and it also, in some products, offers relief from the tax burden they could bear.

Many of the products available have been described above, particularly in chapter 3 and chapter 4. The products described below are those which have extra advantages or come as packages in which products already described can be bought.

The magic of compound interest has been regularly mentioned throughout this book. The sooner that saving starts, the better the result. It has been calculated that, given a scenario where the same amount is saved monthly over 40 years and the same rate of return is added throughout, the sum available at the end of the 40 years from the savings made in the first ten years is slightly more than the sum available from the next 30 years' savings. However,

there can be factors, particularly tax (see Section 2 below), that change the sums and make savings worthwhile even if it has not been possible to start early.

2.1 Individual Savings Accounts (ISAs)

Learning Objective 9.1.1

ISAs and Junior ISAs are tax-exempt ways of saving cash; an ISA lets you put money into different types of investments, such as cash and collective investment schemes. This means your investment can go down as well as up

ISAs are tax-assisted savings accounts. Interest is exempt from income tax and dividends are exempt from higher rate tax, while capital gains are free of capital gains tax (CGT). Basically, nothing that happens in an ISA needs to be reported to the tax authorities (though they do keep a close eye on ISAs to make sure that investors do not cheat).

Investors have an annual subscription limit (from July 2014, this is £15,000) which must be subscribed within the tax year (6 April to 5 April) or lost. Children can subscribe to the Junior ISA which has a lower subscription limit but has largely the same investment rules. Subscriptions can be invested in a wide range of products, such as deposits, stocks and shares, collective investments and insurance policies. These are, of course, subject to the risks and rewards described in chapter 3.

2.2 Government-Guaranteed Savings Products

Learning Objective 9.1.2

National Savings & Investments (NS&I): Premium Bonds and savings accounts

The UK government borrows most of the money it needs from the wholesale markets, in particular the bond market. However, it also borrows from the retail market, in other words from the general public. It makes a range of savings and deposit accounts available, all of which enjoy the government guarantee of repayment and are regarded as absolutely safe as there is no risk that the government will fail to redeem them as promised. However, they still suffer the risk that inflation will destroy some or all of their value (see Section 2.1 in Chapter 2 above). Some of them are only available to a target market such as children or senior citizens. Some products are free of income tax though the interest rate reflects the benefit by being lower than that available in the general market so most of these are particularly beneficial to higher tax payers.

The UK government's most popular and best-known product is the Premium Bonds. Premium Bonds pay no interest but instead are entered into a draw every month for prizes ranging from £25 to £1 million. These prizes are free of tax and the prize fund reflects the interest available on the general market, reduced because of the tax-free nature of the prize. They can be regarded as a lottery, except that the investment is not lost but can always be cashed in. The odds against winning any prize in the monthly draw are 26,000 to 1 while the odds against winning the £1 million prize are 4 billion to 1.

2.3 Life Assurance

Learning Objective 9.1.3

As well as protecting themselves against accidental death, savers can take out life assurance policies that pay out guaranteed sums on retirement

Assurance is protection against things that will happen (ie, death) but you hope not yet, while insurance gives protection against things that could happen but, you hope, never will (eg, fire, theft). Many life assurance products act as a savings mechanism whilst also giving a measure of protection against premature death. They can be used on maturity to do a number of things like pay off a mortgage, assist with school fees, boost retirement savings or pay inheritance tax, amongst others. The policy can be written in trust, allowing it to pass

to children without being included in the estate for inheritance tax purposes.

Life assurance has had a bad press over the last decade as the returns indicated when the policies were taken out failed to materialise, due to the fall in interest rates, the failure of the stock market to produce the level of capital gains that had occurred in the decades leading up to the time they were taken out and changes in the tax treatment of life policies and premiums. However, the mixture of saving and protection continues to give it a role in financial planning.

3. Pensions

Learning Objective 9.2

Pensions provide a regular income for people after retirement

Pensions are designed to provide an income in retirement. In theory, workers forego, or save, a part of their wages/salary during their working life to use in retirement. To encourage this, the state does not tax the money when it is originally paid into the pension but only when it is drawn down in retirement. For a basic rate taxpayer, this means that every 80p in salary saved becomes £1 immediately within the pension, a 25% increase. For higher rate taxpayers the benefit is even more marked as 60p becomes £1 (a 67% increase) while for a top rate taxpayer, 55p becomes £1 (an 82% increase). For those who achieve it, higher rate tax is more likely to be paid towards the end of a career and the benefit of saving what would be otherwise highly taxed can offset the shorter time that compound interest can work its magic.

Pensions are not the only way to save for retirement though they are the most tax-efficient way. ISAs, life assurance, general savings, the house, can all play a part and the sensible will use all the options they can to ensure that they are comfortable at the end of their life.

3.1 Basic State Pension

Learning Objective 9.2.1

Provided they have built up sufficient National Insurance Contributions over their working lives, retirees are paid a pension by the state. It covers around half of the estimated living costs for a retired person, so additional pension provision is considered essential

All those in the UK who qualify by building up sufficient National Insurance Contributions (NICs) over their working life will receive the basic state pension. The contributions can be made as part of the tax deducted from the pay packet, allotted as part of the benefit received for motherhood or unemployment or purchased by subscribing extra. The pension is calculated on a weekly basis but usually paid four weekly and is taxable.

The state pension is designed to prevent the elderly from starving to death but is not enough for a luxurious or even comfortable existence. The current basic pension will bring in a little under £6,000 a year compared with an annual income for someone on the minimum wage of around £10,500. Although the proposed pension changes for 2015 will raise the basic pension to the same level as someone on the maximum pension credit state benefit, or £7,500 a year, the real benefit of the change will be that the pension will not be reduced to take account of savings. It will therefore be beneficial to save even modestly.

There is also doubt as to at what age the state pension will be paid. The pension age was 65 for men and 60 for women. This is being increased in steps so that men and women will, in due course, both receive it at 68. Given the pressure on state finances and the increase in life expectancy (when the state pension was introduced, life expectancy was in the low 60s – it is now in the low 80s), there are rumours that the date at which this will happen will be brought forward and the age increased. It therefore makes sense to regard the state pension as a nice little extra but make your main retirement financial arrangements yourself.

3.2 National Employment Savings Trust (NEST)

Learning Objective 9.2.2

All employees in the UK are now enrolled automatically in a workplace pension scheme. The aim is to help people make up for the shortcomings of the basic state pension

Employers have been obliged to offer their employees a pension arrangement for many years. Recently, the emphasis has been changed so that most employees, depending on age and salary, who formerly had to apply to join, now are automatically enrolled unless they opt out. Employers can use any suitable pension provider but the National Employment Savings Trust (NEST) is a state-backed pension provider that is the default provider. Both employer and employee are obliged to subscribe so that anyone opting out will lose a part of their remuneration.

The objective of the legislation is to encourage employees to save seriously for their retirement and to make it easier for them to do so. Pensions are generally considered boring until it is discovered that you do not have a large enough one, by which time it is too late to do anything about it. By making the emphasis an opt-out one, rather than an opt-in one, the government considered that more workers would acquire a personal pension, if only because it is too much like hard work to make the decision to opt out. The indications are that the government is being proved correct.

3.3 Other Pension Schemes

Learning Objective 9.2.3

Employers may offer other, so-called occupational pensions schemes for their employees. Some of these require the employee to contribute part of their wages or salary to the pension scheme. Individuals can also set up their own personal pension schemes

NEST is only one of a wide variety of pension schemes. The 'gold plated' scheme, or most desirable, is the final salary scheme, which is calculated as a proportion of the final salary earned, depending on the number of years worked in the organisation and is inflation-linked. They are also called defined benefit schemes since it is the amount of benefit that the retiree will get that is fixed, and not the amount that it costs to provide the pension for which the employer is responsible. However, the increase in costs for these schemes, due to the increase in longevity, has meant the greater tax burden introduced in 1997, the increased regulatory burden and the fall in returns due to low interest rates have made them too expensive for most employers to contemplate. As a result, these are largely confined to state employees where the taxpayer pays the bill.

The other type of pension is called 'defined contribution' scheme since the contribution is fixed and the eventual pension is dependent on the performance of the investments in it. These can be either occupational or personal schemes. The former are chosen by the employers, who will usually contribute to it, thus boosting the pension, though the employee can also contribute. The pension is managed by a pension fund manager and is usually invested in collective funds. NEST is a defined contribution scheme.

Personal pensions belong solely to the saver. They are particularly useful for those whose employer does not provide a fund, the self-employed and those who change employment regularly. These must be provided by a registered pension fund but the range of investment options provided give a great deal of flexibility. This flexibility is likely to increase when pension changes proposed in the 2014 budget come into effect in 2015.

4. Annuities (The Pension Pot)

Learning Objective 9.3

Most pension schemes aim to build up a pension 'pot', which upon retirement can be sold to a financial services provider in return for a sum of money paid annually. This payment is called an annuity

The great day has arrived, the managing director has shaken your hand and said some nice words about your contribution to the company and you are retired. Since you no longer have a salary, you are reliant on your pension pot – the funds you have been saving for so many years – to provide you with an income. What can you do with the pot? How do you ensure that you can afford to do all the exciting things you want to do?

The first 25% of the pot can be drawn down free of tax. Even for a basic rate taxpayer, this increases the amount that can be drawn down by a quarter and for higher taxpayers, the concession is even more valuable. The funds can be spent, but also used as an available investment, for instance in an ISA, or to pay off debt such as a mortgage.

4.1 Annuities and Life Expectancy

Learning Objective 9.3.1

The longer the provider expects the annuity buyer to live, the lower will be the annual payment offered and vice versa. That is why smokers and other people with impaired life expectancy can expect higher annuity rates

The traditional home for a pension pot has always been an annuity. Indeed, for most pensioners, it has been obligatory under the regulations. An annuity is a regular, annual income, purchased with the pension pot. It can be flat (in other words, the same each year) or inflation-linked and the amount paid reflects this, with inflation-linked being a much lower figure initially, though the pensioner hopes that in due course it will rise to compensate him for price inflation.

Annuities are a bet with the provider because, on death, no more is paid out and any remains of the pension pot stays with the insurance company providing the annuity. The longer the pensioner lives, the better the bargain he has, and the worse for the provider. Most annuities are provided by insurance companies who welcome early deaths for the additional profit they bring. Because of this gamble of life and death, insurance companies will give better rates to pensioners in poor health and smokers. Annuity providers have been keeping statistics on death rates since the early 18th century but the recent increase in life expectancy has surprised even them.

This increase, together with the precipitous fall in interest rates and the indifferent performance of stock exchange securities, have reduced annuity rates significantly, so that anyone retiring now is likely to receive a much lower annuity for the same size pension pot than someone who retired 20 years ago, perhaps less than half.

4.2 Draw Down

The Chancellor of the Exchequer announced the biggest change in pension rules in 50 years in the 2014 budget. As mentioned in Section 3.1, it is currently obligatory for pensioners to use their pension pot to purchase an annuity, thus guaranteeing that they have an income for life and are less likely to become a charge on the taxpayer. This will all change in 2015 when new rules come into effect, which will allow pensioners to draw down their pensions as and when they want.

Drawdown has always been available but only permitted to those who can prove that they have a sufficient income elsewhere, such as a defined benefit pension paying over £12,000. The rules have always been written with a view to ensuring that pensioners do not become a drain on the state. The current rules on drawdown also reflect this. Apart from the tax-free 25%, only a maximum stipulated amount can be withdrawn each year.

Under the new rules, pensioners will be able to withdraw money from their pension as and when they want, thus implying that investors who have saved carefully all their lives are unlikely to blow the lot on a Lamborghini just because the rules allow them to. This will allow much greater flexibility, particularly with the less defined lifestyle we now have. When the pension rules were written, retirement was an end to employment. Now, it may be a change of style but may still involve elements of paid work that mean that a full pension is not required. Alternatively, where it is likely that the pensioner will not live long due to illness, funds can be drawn down more quickly.

It is likely that annuities will still be the home for a major part of pension savings as a guaranteed lifetime income will still be very attractive. However, this will be the decision of the pensioner, not the state.

5. Wills

Making a will should be part of everyone's long term planning, along with career, children, pension saving and the next holiday. It is sometimes thought of as admitting weakness and vulnerability. It is actually a sign of maturity and good sense. Anyone with assets and/or dependents should make a will and keep it up-to-date. Failing to do so, should the worst happen, means that the rules of intestacy (meaning no will) apply. Only wives, civil partners and blood relatives are regarded as having an interest, however long a relationship may have existed. For example, the writer of the Millennium series of books (Girl with a Dragon Tattoo, etc.), one of the most successful and therefore profitable series of books in the last decade, died suddenly at the age of 50 without making a valid will. His much loved partner of 20 years received nothing and all his money went to his family, whom he disliked intensely and to whom he had not spoken for years. Even where the deceased was married, the intestacy rules will split the estate in ways that can make life difficult.

Making a will does not mean that it will be needed for years, or that it cannot be changed. Indeed, a marriage nullifies any will made before it. However, should the worst happen, it means that children will be looked after as you want, and not as the social services dictate, and your loved ones will remember you with love and not annoyance.

📄 Chapter Questions

Based on what you have learned in Chapter Nine, try to answer the following questions.

Think of an answer for each question and refer to the appropriate section for confirmation.

1. What tax benefits are available to ISA investors?

    Answer reference: Section 2.1

    ....

    ....

2. What are the two main benefits of life assurance?

    Answer reference: Section 2.3

    ....

3. Since the UK Government provides a state pension, why should workers also save for one?

    Answer reference: Section 3.1

    ....

    ....

4. What are the benefits and drawbacks of a pension that can be drawn down without restriction?

    Answer reference: Section 4.2

    ....

    ....

5. Why is making a will important?

    Answer reference: Section 5

    ....

The Ethics of Business

10

1. Looking After Money   109

2. Managing a Company   110

3. The Government   111

4. Crime and Scams   111

This syllabus area will provide approximately 3 of the 30 examination questions

The Ethics of Business

Learning Objective 10

Stewardship is the concept of looking after someone's property as if it were one's own

1. Looking After Money

Financial services involves the looking after of investors' money. To do so on a long-term basis requires a level of trust that has to be earned over years, if not decades. The question to be asked by any manager, adviser or administrator in the industry, before making a decision, is *'would I make this decision this way if it were my own money?'*. In other words, they must put the interest of their customers ahead of their own personal benefit.

In fact, a reputation for honesty and integrity can be worth money in the bank. The reputation of the John Lewis Partnership was mentioned in Chapter 7, Section 4. Unfortunately for the financial services industry, a number of scandals involving mis-selling and mismanagement, such as personal pensions, endowment insurance and the 2007 financial crash, seriously reduced the high standing the industry had previously earned even if not all the blame was deserved. When this happens, an industry has to ensure that it is even more visibly honest if it is to restore its reputation. Unfortunately, it only takes a few bad apples to ruin a barrel full of good ones.

1.1 Trust

Learning Objective 10.1

When people entrust their life savings to others, they have a right to expect the highest levels of due care and attention. That is why financial service providers have a duty of stewardship

The assets of customers of financial services companies are held in trust. This means that they are held separately from the assets of the company looking after them and are frequently placed with a third party, which is charged with keeping them safe and ensuring that they are not misused or stolen. Customers can expect that, when they place assets with a company, they will receive them back at maturity.

The good governance that financial services companies should follow is reinforced by regulation. As well as guiding companies in what they should do, the regulations change what could once been regarded as just an error into a criminal act that can be punished through the courts or by the regulators. However, too much regulation and an emphasis on the detail can mean that companies and regulators spend too much time checking that the detail of the rules are complied with and can miss the big picture. Many of the decisions that caused the 2007 crash were signed off by compliance, legal teams and the regulators as legal and in line with the regulations, as indeed they were. The fact that some of them were, with the benefit of hindsight, stupid was completely missed.

1.2 Customers

Learning Objective 10.1.1

The customers of financial services providers have a right to be treated fairly. The UK's financial regulation system is focused on this aim

Learning Objective 10.1.2

The customers of financial services providers have a right to be treated fairly. The UK's financial regulation system is focused on this aim

The relationship between customer and company should be one of trust and mutual good faith. The financial services company should treat customers fairly and communicate with them in a way that is clear and not misleading. They should aim to produce a good service or product at a reasonable price.

Customers should also treat the relationship as being one based on the utmost good faith. Information given should be accurate and truthful. Customers should also accept that firms need to make an adequate profit and pay directors and staff in line with what is deserved. It is better to have a company that is able to continue to serve customers than one that collapses half way a through contract by going bust.

2. Managing a Company

Learning Objective 10.2

Directors of companies are entrusted by the shareholders to run the company in a prudent but profitable way; but many others have a stake in the way in which a company is run

Directors have a legal obligation to run the company they lead in the best interests of the owners – the shareholders. The shareholders also have a responsibility for calling the directors to account at the annual general meeting, approving their management of the company over the last year and, if necessary, dispensing with their services.

However, shareholders are not the only ones with an interest in the company. There are a number of other stakeholders, all of whom have an interest in the good running of the company but with different view as to how the benefits of a well-run profitable company should be allocated. It is the directors' responsibility to balance these competing interests and decide how the company should go forward.

2.1 Stakeholders

Learning Objective 10.2.1

Stakeholders in a company include shareholders, employees, customers, and the government. They all rely on the directors and managers to run the company well

Learning Objective 10.2.2

The directors and managers of companies should not enrich themselves at the expense of their stakeholders

Apart from directors and shareholders, other stakeholders include employees, customers, suppliers, the government and the local communities near the company's production facilities and offices. All of these would prefer the benefits to be skewed in their direction and will use their best efforts to achieve this end. At the end of the day, all should want the company to be successful and continue to provide the benefits that all stakeholders have come to expect, though sometimes stakeholders can be remarkably short-sighted and even capable of activity that could destroy the company. It is up to the directors to decide how the benefits should be distributed, within the parameters permitted by law.

Directors and senior managers are often in a position to direct an excessive share of the benefits to themselves and must make sure that they do not enrich themselves unduly at the expense of other stakeholders. On the other hand, star performers who add significantly to the profits of the company through their efforts and skill not only deserve a share of that extra profit, but also could leave for pastures new if they do not get it, to the detriment of the company. One way of retaining the stars is by the use of bonuses. These allow the company to offer a lower base salary and to give bonuses only when the star's personal efforts deserve it. It is also possible to structure bonuses so that they are paid some time after the profits are made, ensuring that the profits are real and to claw the bonus money back should it be found that the profits disappear with time.

3. The Government

Learning Objective 10.3

The government has responsibility to its citizens to use state funds wisely and fairly

Learning Objective 10.3.1

As a consequence of the financial crisis of 2007–08, several banks are now owned by the government. The government has a duty to ensure that these banks provide a return for the tax-payer, while also performing their commercial function of taking deposits and lending to firms and individuals

The government is a major stakeholder in all companies, as taxman, regulator, legislator and, in some companies, shareholder. It has to balance out its responsibility to achieve its economic targets with its desire to gain social benefits for voters. For instance, adjusting the level of tax payable by companies may reduce the percentage paid by each company while increasing the total tax paid by making the UK a more attractive place to do business. The result of a policy change may easily be counter-intuitive but is not always so. In particular, the Government acquired stakes in two major banks, the Royal Bank of Scotland (RBS) and Lloyds, following the 2007 financial crash. It has

CHARTERED INSTITUTE FOR
SECURITIES & INVESTMENT

to be careful in these cases that it does not allow its desire to use the banks to forward its policy targets, for instance by promoting lending to unsuitable borrowers, to be at the expense of its responsibility to ensure a decent return for the taxpayer who put up the initial money.

4. Crime and Scams

It is unfortunate that wherever there is money, those with criminal intent are inclined to gather. Financial services are, as the name implies, all about money. Any criminal activity within the major companies, should there be any, is best left to the regulators and the police. This section is about those criminals who target ordinary people and who have no connection with any reputable organisation, though they may try to persuade the gullible that they do.

The basic rule of thumb is that if it sounds too good to be true, it is too good to be true. This is reinforced if the contact says that it is necessary to pay money up front as expenses before the jackpot/lottery win/inheritance is released. This type of crime is known as front-end fee fraud since the criminals' target is to obtain the fee. One particularly successful fraudster pretended to sell manure in Bahrain, taking a deposit for each 'deal'. By the time he disappeared with the deposit money, he had sold sufficient manure to cover the whole of Bahrain to the depth of eight foot!

Criminals have become adept at changing their tactics and the growth of the internet has given them an immense new field in which to practice their frauds' on. It has also allowed them new ways of extracting money from their victims. Obtaining the victim's bank account details,

together with their PINs, is the equivalent of being handed the contents of the account.

The following is intended to give guidance on the do's and don'ts of keeping clear of becoming a victim. Remember that criminals are always finding new stories and new approaches.

- Treat any cold call or unsolicited approach as suspicious, particularly if money comes up in the conversation. Reputable financial organisations are not permitted to make cold calls. Indeed, it can be a criminal offence in the UK, which is why so many criminals call from abroad.
- Never give details of your bank account, PIN or any passwords to a cold caller. Your bank will never ask for these details in a call to you (they have this knowledge anyway). If you call them, they will only ask for a part of your PIN or password, not the whole of it.
- If you are asked to call back, always make sure you have a dialling tone before you do. Fraudsters will keep the line open and will pretend to be your bank or the police, if you dial back without a tone.
- If they claim to be regulated in the UK, ask for their FCA number and check it on http://www.fsa.gov.uk/register/home.do. Then contact the firm, using the number on their basic details on the FCA website.
- If it sounds dodgy and dishonest, don't touch it. It is probably a scam at best or involves criminal action at worst. Criminals are not only keen to help themselves to their victims' cash but also to use them to transfer cash out of the country and money launder it. This can land anyone fooled into a jail sentence.

It is worth keeping an eye on fraud in general at http://www.actionfraud.police.uk/ and financial fraud in particular on http://www.fca.org.uk/consumers/scams.

If things go wrong, and it is not your fault, when dealing with reputable regulated firms, there are a host of organisations ready to help correct errors, including the FCA and other regulators and various ombudsmen. If it happens outside the system, then you are on your own! The police will be more interested in placing the criminals in jail than in recovering any money you might have lost.

📄 Chapter Questions

Based on what you have learned in Chapter Ten, try to answer the following questions.

Think of an answer for each question and refer to the appropriate section for confirmation.

1. Why is trust important in financial services?

    Answer reference: Section 1.1

    ....

    ....

2. What should a supplier/customer relationship be based on?

    Answer reference: Section 1.2

    ....

    ....

3. What are the stakeholders in a company?

    Answer reference: Section 2

    ....

    ....

4. How can the government be a stakeholder in financial Services companies?

    Answer reference: Section 3

    ....

    ....

5. How are criminals attracted to financial services?

    Answer reference: Section 4

    ....

    ....

Glossary and Abbreviations

Annual Equivalent Rate (AER)

The annualised compound rate of interest applied to a cash deposit or to a loan. Also known as the Effective Annual Rate.

Annual Percentage Rate (APR)

Basic annual interest rate without taking account of compounding.

Annuity

Annual income purchased with a lump sum and paid until death.

Asset

Any item of economic or financial value owned by someone or a company.

Assurance

Policy protecting against financial losses due to death. Also used for saving.

Balance Sheet

A summary of a company's assets (what it owns), liabilities (what it owes), and owner's equity at the end of a financial year.

Bank of England

The UK's central bank. Implements economic policy decided by the Treasury and determines interest rates.

Bankrupt

The situation where an individual, company or other organisation is unable to pay its debts.

Barter

An exchange of goods or services, largely superseded by money.

Bonds

Interest-bearing securities which entitle holders to annual interest and repayment at maturity. Commonly issued by companies and governments.

Broker

An individual who handles orders to buy and sell from its investors or clients. Brokers often charge a commission for the work they perform. A broker who specialises in stocks, bonds or options acts as an agent and must be registered with the exchange where the securities are traded. Brokers in financial services also commonly need to be regulated by the local financial services regulator.

Capital

Cash and assets used to generate income or make an investment.

Capital Gain

An increase in the market value of a security (ie, the value of the asset is greater than the price they were bought for).

Central Bank

Central banks typically have responsibility for setting a nation's or a region's short-term interest rate, controlling the money supply, acting as banker and lender of last resort to the banking system and managing the national debt.

Collective Investment Scheme (CIS)

A fund run by a professional manager that enables investors to pool their money. The manager selects the investments and the investors share in any increase (or decrease) in their value.

Commodity

Raw material (for example, oil, gold, wheat) traded on a market dedicated to that particular commodity.

Compound Interest

When interest is paid on interest as well as the capital sum. Only occurs when interest is not withdrawn/spent.

Credit Balances

Positive amount held on a bank account.

Credit Rating

An assessment of a bond issuer's ability to pay the interest and repay the capital on the bonds. The best rating is triple A.

Currency

Any form of money that circulates in an economy as an accepted means of exchange for goods and services.

Dealer

An individual or firm acting in order to buy or sell a security for its own account and risk.

Default

The situation where a borrower has failed to meet the requirements of their borrowing, for example by failing to pay the interest due.

Deflation

Fall in prices, often due to lack of demand in an economic depression.

Deposit

A deposit is a sum of money held at a financial institution on behalf of an account holder for safekeeping.

Diversification

Investment strategy involving spreading risk by investing in a range of investments.

Dividend

Distribution of profits by a company.

Dividend Yield

Most recent dividend expressed as a percentage of current share price.

Equity

Another name for shares or stock. It can also be used to refer to the amount by which the value of a house exceeds any mortgage or borrowings secured on it.

Exchange

Marketplace for trading investments.

Exchange Rate

Rate at which one currency can be exchanged for another.

Financial Conduct Authority (FCA)

Regulator charged with monitoring and guiding the conduct of business between firms and customers and between firms and firms in the UK.

Fiscal

Relating to tax and taxation

Fixed-Rate Mortgage

A loan at a fixed rate of interest used to buy a house and secured on the property, which can be sold by the lender to repay the loan if the terms are not adhered to.

Foreign Exchange Market

The market for the trading of foreign currencies.

Forex

Abbreviation for foreign exchange trading.

Forward Transaction

A sale or purchase transaction for future delivery, often used for foreign exchange or commodities.

Fracking

Extracting gas and oil from the ground by injecting water and chemicals

FTSE 100 ('Footsie')

Main UK share index of 100 leading shares.

Fund Manager

Firm that invests money on behalf of customers.

Gearing

The effect of purchasing property or investments using borrowed money on the increase of profits or losses. Alternatively, the impact on profit brought about by a change in revenue for a company having a high proportion of fixed costs.

Gross

Total amount before deductions (ie, taxes).

Index

A statistical measure of the changes in a selection of stocks representing a portion of the overall market.

Individual Savings Accounts (ISAs)

Tax-assisted method of saving and investing in deposit accounts, securities and shares.

Inflation

An increase in the general level of prices.

Insurance

Policy protecting against the financial losses involved with disasters such as fire and theft and accidents which it is hoped will never happen. (Also see *Assurance*)

Interest

The price paid for borrowing money, or received for depositing money. Generally, interest is expressed as a percentage rate over a period of time, such as 5% per annum.

Intermediary

Agent, market, organisation or institution standing between two sides of a transaction.

Limited Company

Company where the shareholders' liability to any losses the company might make is limited to the money they have subscribed.

Liquidity

The ease with which an item can be traded on the market. Liquid markets are described as 'deep'.

Liquidity Risk

The risk that an asset may be difficult to sell at a reasonable price.

Lloyd's of London

Market place for the placing and transfer of insurance risk.

Loan

A form of debt where a borrower receives a certain amount of money from a lender. The borrower agrees to pay a contracted rate of interest to the lender and also agrees a date on which the loan will be repaid.

London Stock Exchange (LSE)

Main UK market for securities.

Market

All exchanges are markets – electronic or physical meeting places where assets are bought and sold.

Market Price

Price of an asset like a share as quoted on the exchange, or established by a market.

Maturity

Date when the capital on a bond is repaid.

Mortgage

A mortgage, or more precisely a mortgage loan, is a long-term loan used to finance the purchase of real estate (eg, a house). Under the mortgage agreement, the borrower agrees to make a series of payments back to the lender. The money lent by the bank (or building society) is secured against the value of the property: if the payments are not made by the borrower, the lender can take back the property.

Mutual Fund

A type of collective investment scheme found in the US.

Nominal Value

The amount of a bond that will be repaid on maturity. Also known as face or par value.

Overdraft

A form of borrowing from a bank where the lending bank can demand repayment at any time.

Patent

Legal protection for inventors allowing them to exploit the benefits of an invention for a fixed number of years.

Pawnbroker

Business that provides loans to individuals. The pawnbroker takes an item of security (such as jewellery) in exchange for the loan. The loan needs to be repaid for the borrower to reclaim the item.

Payday Loan

Very short-term loan that needs to be repaid on the borrower's next payday, usually the end of the month. Such loans are often very expensive.

Pension Fund

A fund set up by a company or government to invest the pension contributions of members and employees to be paid out at retirement age.

Personal Loan

A loan taken out by an individual where the precise purpose for which the money will be used is not detailed in the loan agreement.

Personal Pension Scheme

A retirement saving scheme set up by an individual, rather than set up by the individual's employer.

Portfolio

A combination of investments.

Premium

The regular payment made to an insurance company for insurance against a range of risks.

Price Earnings Ratio

Way of measuring the value of shares where the share price is divided by the earnings (profit) per share.

Public Limited Company

A limited company (see above) where the shares are often widely held and usually quoted on a stock exchange.

Redemption Date

The date at which a bond issuer has to repay the face value of the bond.

Reinsurance

The term for insurance taken out by an insurer on a policy that it has underwritten.

Return

A measure of the financial reward on an investment, such as dividends and capital growth on a share. Return is always linked to risk: to have the possibility of a bigger reward, a bigger risk will need to be taken.

Secured

The situation where a lender (such as a bank or a pawnbroker) takes something of value. If the borrower fails to repay the debt, the lender is able to keep and sell the item.

Securities

Bonds and equities.

Security

A bank has taken security for its loan when it holds something of value. The most obvious example is where a bank takes security in the form of property ownership on a mortgage.

Shareholders

Those who own the shares of the company. Essentially, they are the owners of the company.

Spot Rate

The rate for a transaction, usually currency for immediate delivery.

Start-Up

A business or company in its early stages. Typically start ups are businesses that are not yet generating any profits.

State Pension Scheme (SPS)

A retirement scheme that is provided by the state. Such schemes are generally not particularly generous and need to be supplemented by other forms of income in retirement (such as personal pension schemes, or pension schemes provided by the employer).

Syndicate

Insurance companies joining together to write insurance, or banks joining together to provide loans.

Trade Marks

A recognisable sign, design or expression which identifies products or services of a particular source from those of others.

Topography

The geographic layout of a country or area, such as mountains, rivers sea and coasts.

Unsecured

A loan provided to a borrower where the lender takes no security.

Yield

Income from an investment as a percentage of the current price.

Abbreviations

AER	Annual Equivalent Rate		**QE**	Quantitative Easing
APR	Annual Percentage Rate		**RBS**	Royal Bank of Scotland
ATM	Automated Teller Machine		**RPI**	Retail Prices Index
CAB	Citizens' Advice Bureau		**VAT**	Value Added Tax
CIS	Collective Investment Scheme			
CPI	Consumer Price Index			
ETF	Exchange-Traded Fund			
EU	European Union			
FCA	Financial Conduct Authority			
GDP	Gross Domestic Product			
IMF	International Monetary Fund			
ISA	Individual Savings Account			
LIBOR	London InterBank Offered Rate			
LSE	London Stock Exchange			
NEST	National Employment Savings Trust			
NIC	National Insurance Contribution			
NINJA	No Income, No job or Assets			
NMS	Normal Market Size			
NS&I	National Savings and Investments			
OEIC	Open Ended Investment Company			
OPEC	Organisation of Petroleum Exporting Countries			
PA	Per Annum			
PIN	Personal Identification Number			
PLC	Public Limited Company			
PRA	Prudential Regulation Authority			

Multiple Choice Questions

Fundamentals of Business and Finance

Multiple Choice Questions

The assessment for this course will be a one-hour examination consisting of 30 multiple choice questions.

The following questions have been compiled to reflect as closely as possible the standard you will experience in your examination. Please note, however, they are not the CISI examination questions themselves.

Tick one answer for each question. When you have completed all questions, refer to the end of this section for the answers.

1.   An increase in supply is likely to:

A. Increase prices

B. Keep prices the same

C. Reduce prices

D. Make prices more variable

2.   If a business requires foreign currency in six months' time, it will deal at which of the following prices?

A. A spot rate

B. An interest rate

C. A forward rate

D. A loan rate

3.   A time of persistently rising prices is known as:

A. reflation

B. deflation

C. inflation

D. conflation

4.   Which of the following is likely to be the cheapest source of borrowing?

A. A pay day lender

B. A credit card

C. A pawn shop

D. An unsecured loan from a bank

5.   **The rewards of investing in shares are:**

   A. dividends
   B. interest
   C. rent
   D. guaranteed return of capital

6.   **Which of the following is NOT considered to be income?**

   A. Interest
   B. Dividends
   C. Capital growth
   D. Rent

7.   **Which of the following risks would typically NOT be insured?**

   A. Fire
   B. Burglary
   C. Investment
   D. Motor

8.   **Which of the following is a closed-ended investment scheme?**

   A. Unit trust
   B. Investment trust
   C. OEIC
   D. ETF

9.   **If the share price is £4.50 and the earnings per share are 15p, then the price earnings ratio is:**

   A. 25
   B. 30
   C. 35
   D. 40

10.   **If the share price is £4.50 and the dividend is 18p per share, then the yield is:**

   A. 3.6%
   B. 4.0%
   C. 4.4%
   D. 4.5%

11. If the Bank of England raises interest rates it is likely that:

A. Consumer expenditure will rise

B. Consumer expenditure will fall

C. Bond prices will rise

D. Retail prices will fall

12. Value Added Tax is:

A. A direct tax

B. An indirect tax

C. A wealth tax

D. A property tax

13. Directors have a legal duty to do which ONE of the following?

A. Minimise energy consumption by the company

B. Run as profitable a company as possible

C. Ensure their fellow directors obey the law

D. Report to shareholders at least four times a year

14. Factors of production describes which ONE of the following?

A. The inputs described by economists for producing goods

B. The cast of a play

C. The mathematical formula for breaking even

D. The end product of a production line

15. Which of the following is not an informal market?

A. Stock market

B. Labour market

C. Lloyds of London

D. Metals Exchange

16. Which of the following is the largest market by daily turnover?

A. Stock exchange

B. Property market

C. Forex market

D. Money market

17. **For which ONE of the following does the UK Government allow savings to be offset against income tax?**

     A. Pensions

     B. ISAs

     C. Premium Bonds

     D. Life Assurance

18. **An annuity is paid:**

     A. For the rest of the annuitant's life

     B. Until the money runs out

     C. Once a year

     D. Only when it is drawn down

19. **In which of the following did the UK Government take a stake following the 2007 financial crash?**

     A. Santander

     B. Lloyds

     C. Barclays

     D. Nationwide

20. **Which of the following is responsible for making laws governing financial services?**

     A. The Bank of England

     B. The Financial Conduct Authority

     C. The Government

     D. The European Economic Authority

Answers to Multiple Choice Questions

Q1.   **Answer: C**   **Ref: Chapter 1, Section 2.4**

An increase in the supply of goods and a continuation of demand at the same level is likely to depress the price.

Q2.   **Answer: C**   **Ref: Chapter 1, Section 4**

When dealing in foreign exchange for delivery at a future time, the business will deal at a forward rate.

Q3.   **Answer: C**   **Ref: Chapter 2, Section 2.1**

A time of rising prices is known as inflation. Deflation is a time of falling prices. Reflation occurs when governments take action to encourage an inactive economy while conflation is not in the dictionary!

Q4.   **Answer: D**   **Ref: Chapter 2, Sections 4.2 & 4.3**

All the sources of finance quoted in this question are likely to be more expensive than a secured loan. However, a formal unsecured loan will probably be the cheapest option. Credit cards vary between 15% and 35%pa, pawn shops will charge more while a pay day lender will charge up to 5,000% pa

Q5.   **Answer: A**   **Ref: Chapter 3, Section 3.3.2**

Investors receive income from shares in the form of dividends. Interest is paid on bonds and deposits, rent on property while there is nothing guaranteed about any growth that may occur to a shareholding.

Q6.   **Answer: C**   **Ref: Chapter C, Section 3.3**

Capital growth is a capital gain and is regarded as either the reward of canny investing or a windfall.

Q7.   **Answer: C**   **Ref: Chapter 4, Section 1**

While it is possible to reduce the risk inherent in investment through diversification, it is not possible to buy insurance policies against the risk that share prices might go down.

Q8.   **Answer: B**   **Ref: Chapter 4, Section 3**

Investment trusts are 'closed ended' funds, meaning that there are a finite number of shares available and the share price depends upon supply and demand. The other three suggestions are 'open ended' and units are created or cancelled to reflect demand.

Q9.   **Answer: B**   **Ref: Chapter 5, Section 3.2**

Share price divided by earnings per share.

450/15.

Q10.   **Answer: B**   **Ref: Chapter 5, Section 3.1**

Dividend per share divided by share price times 100.

18/450 x 100 = 4.0%

Q11.   **Answer: B**   **Ref: Chapter 6, Section 1.1.1**

The Bank of England's action will mean that interest rates are raised where possible by lenders, particularly for mortgages. If more of the family budget is going to pay the mortgage, there will be less for other things and consumer expenditure will fall.

Q12.   **Answer: B**   **Ref: Chapter 6, Section 2.1**

VAT is paid on expenditure and is therefore not charged on wealth or property. Each VAT charge is paid through a number of intermediaries, such as a shop-wholesaler-manufacturer so it is indirect. Direct taxes are paid direct to HMRC.

Q13.   **Answer: B**   **Ref: Chapter 7, Section 4**

Although Directors will carry out all the duties described in this question, it is only the requirement to run a profitable company that is a legal duty specifically of Directors.

Q14.   **Answer: A**   **Ref: Chapter 7, Section 2**

Factors of production are the inputs described by economists when discussing the production of goods.

Q15.   **Answer: B**   **Ref: Chapter 8, Section 2**

The Labour Market is an informal market. The other markets listed are formal markets.

Q16.   **Answer: C**   **Ref: Chapter 8, Section 2.4.2**

The Forex market (Foreign Exchange Market) is the largest market, with a daily turnover of $5 trillion.

Q17.   **Answer: D**   **Ref: Chapter 9, Sections 1 & 2**

Pension saving is the only one where the saving itself is offsettable by tax. The other forms all have some form of tax benefit but only after the saving has been made.

Q18.   **Answer: A**   **Ref: Chapter 9, Section 3.1**

An annuity is paid for the rest of an annuitant's life. It is a bet against the provider's estimate as to how long the annuitant will live. No matter how long he or she does live, the provider is contracted to keep paying.

Q19.   **Answer: B**   **Ref: Chapter 10, Section 3**

The Government acquired stakes in RBS and Lloyds following the 2007 financial crash.

Q20.   **Answer: C**   **Ref: Chapter 10, Section 3**

The Government is responsible for making all laws in UK.

Syllabus Learning Map

Syllabus Unit/ Element		Chapter/ Section
ELEMENT 1	**Buying and Selling**	Chapter 1
	Candidates must know that price is established by the interaction of buyers and sellers. In all markets – including those for financial products – traders try to profit from the difference between the buying price and selling price	
1.1	**Specialisation and trade** How specialisation has led to a need for a system of trade; how a trading system based on barter gave way to a system based on money	2.1
1.1.1	**Price** How money has made price the basis of trade and how markets enable buyers and sellers to come together	2.2
1.1.2	**Supply and demand** How wants are unlimited and resources are scarce; how markets establish a balance between those wants and the supply of resources to satisfy them	2.4
1.1.3	**Pricing mechanism in markets** How price will adjust to the level at which demand is willing to buy and supply is willing to sell; how price signals that a good or service is in short or plentiful supply	2.4
1.2	**Saving and borrowing** How a trading system based on money leads to the build-up of surpluses (more money than people need for their day-today expenses) and deficits (not enough money for day-to-day expenses)	**3**
1.2.1	**Savers – surplus money** How savers (who have surplus money) seek to earn a return on their spare cash by charging interest.	3.1
1.2.2	**Borrowers – shortage of money** How borrowers (who are short of money) have to pay interest to those who are willing to lend it to them.	3.2
1.2.3	**Lending spread** How banks and building societies work as intermediaries between savers and borrowers and charge a higher rate for lending to borrowers than they pay out to the savers	3.4
1.3	**Foreign exchange** How the system of foreign exchange markets allows one currency to be exchanged for another to facilitate international trade	**4**
1.3.1	**Exchange rates** How most currencies in the world move up and down in relation to other currencies	4.1

Syllabus Unit/ Element		Chapter/ Section
1.3.2	**Currency trading** How foreign exchange transactions are conducted; how a foreign exchange dealer makes a profit by selling a currency at a higher price and buying the currency back at a lower price	4
1.3.3	**How supply and demand for currencies affect exchange rates** How strong demand for a currency will push up its 'price' relative to other currencies and weaker demand will pull its 'price' down	4.1
1.4	**The fundamentals of trading** How the desire for profit will encourage buyers to try to pay as low a price as possible and sellers to charge as high a price as possible	**5**
1.4.1	**Bid/Offer spreads** In a normal market, traders will always seek to sell a product a price which is higher than the price they paid to acquire that product in the first place	5
1.4.2	**Profits from trading** Trading is usually profitable if the gap (or "spread") between the buying price and selling price is wide enough	5.1
1.4.3	**Narrow and wide spreads** The size of the spread is the trader's profit margin. The narrower the spread, the less profit the trader is likely to make; the wider the spread, the more profit	5.2
1.5	**Trading of shares and other securities** Companies sell shares to members of the public in return for investment capital	**6**
1.5.1	**Secondary market in shares** Shares can be bought and sold on stock exchanges. The selling price will nearly always be higher than the buying price	6.2

ELEMENT 2	**THE VALUE OF MONEY NOW AND IN THE FUTURE**	Chapter 2
	Money in our pocket today is valued more highly than the promise of the same amount of money in the future. This is due to time preference and the desire to avoid erosion of buying power by inflation	
2.1	**Buy now or pay later?** Goods or services available now are preferred to otherwise identical goods available in the future	**1**
2.1.1	**Time preference** People are prepared to pay more to have the use of a good or service immediately, rather than wait to save up for it – hence the popularity of credit cards	1.1

Syllabus Unit/ Element		Chapter/ Section
2.1.2	**Opportunity cost** Money available now can be invested to generate income; if the money is tied up elsewhere for a long time, that missed opportunity is a cost	1.2
2.2	**Inflation** What inflation is and how it erodes the value of financial assets	**2.2**
2.2.1	**Definition of inflation** A general increase in the level of prices	2.1
2.2.2	**Erosion of buying power** How inflation erodes the buying power of money over time	2.2
2.2.3	**Use of indices to measure inflation** How to construct a basic binary index	2.4
2.2.4	**CPI** How governments use CPI to measure the impact of inflation on their citizens	2.5
2.3	**Interest** Interest is the price of money. It can be described as the 'rent' that owners of money charge for lending out their money; it compensates them for time preference and the risk of inflation	**3**
2.3.1	**Calculation of interest** Know how to calculate: simple interest and Annual Percentage Rate (APR)	3.1
2.3.2	**Compound interest** Know how to calculate Annual Equivalent Rate (AER)	3.2
2.4	**Types of borrowing; costs of borrowing** Know that banks and other financial institutions offer many different borrowing products to individuals	**4**
2.4.1	**Borrowing from banks: loans and overdrafts** Understand the difference between fixed term loans and overdrafts, which can be withdrawn at any time	4.1
2.4.2	**Borrowing from other sources: credit cards, pay-day lenders** Understand the characteristics of credit cards and pay-day loans; how outstanding balances can quickly build up	4.3
2.4.3	**Secured and unsecured borrowing** Borrowers can offer to the lender a valuable possession (ie, an asset) as security that the loan will be repaid. A mortgage is a loan secured on the property being purchased	4.2
2.4.4	**Relationship between loan size and cost of borrowing** Loans incur administration costs for lenders irrespective of the size of the loan: a loan for a large sum of money is there more cost effective for lenders, allowing them to offer an otherwise lower rate of interest to the borrower	4.5

Syllabus Unit/ Element		Chapter/ Section
2.4.5	**Bonds Governments and large companies borrow** money in return for IOUs called 'bonds'. These loans are usually for large amounts and usually have a fixed term of several years' duration and carry a fixed rate of interest	4.4

ELEMENT 3	RISK AND REWARD	Chapter 3
	People face financial risks in the course of their everyday lives. They also risk losing their money when they invest it. The level of risk varies according to the type of investment. The anticipated reward from making an investment should reflect the level of risk attached to it: the greater the risk, the greater the reward required by the investor to compensate for that risk	
3.1	**Personal financial risks** Individuals face financial risk in the everyday course of their lives	**1.1**
3.1.1	**Risk of loss of personal assets** Risk to personal assets, such as homes, household possessions or cars etc, from accidental damage, fire or theft	1.2
3.1.2	Earnings risk Risk to earnings from ill health, injury or accidental death	1.3
3.1.3	**Risk of being held liable for causing financial loss to others** Causing third parties to suffer injury or death; causing damage to third parties' property	1.4
3.2	**The risk of investment** Any investment, from buying one's own home to buying shares in a company, carries additional risks	**2**
3.2.1	**Price risk** The price of financial assets and other assets (such as property) can fall	2.1
3.2.2	**Liquidity risk** Liquidity means the ease with which an investment can be converted back into cash. It may be difficult to convert an investment into cash if the market has insufficient buyers and sellers (ie, it is illiquid)	2.3
3.2.3	**Issuer risk (default risk)** The company that issues shares or bonds (or the bank or building society that accepts deposits) might go bankrupt and be unable to repay investors in full.	2.5
3.3	**The rewards of investment** Investment is rewarded in three main ways: interest; dividend; capital gain. Sometimes it can be a combination of more than one of these types of reward	**3**

Syllabus Unit/ Element		Chapter/ Section
3.3.1	**Interest** Interest compensates the owner of the money for: not being able to spend it on other things immediately; for future erosion of the value of the money by inflation; for the risk that the money might not be repaid	3.1
3.3.2	**Dividends** Shareholders receive a return on the capital they invest in companies in the form of dividends – a proportionate share of the company's distributed profits	3.2
3.3.3	**Capital gain** Capital gain results from an increase in the market value of the investment	3.4
3.4	**Relationship between risk and reward** Lenders (and investors) will always seek higher returns to compensate them for higher risk	**4**
3.4.1	**Long-term vs short-term investments** The longer money is tied up in an investment, the greater the chance that something can go wrong. This will be reflected in a higher return being offered to investors	4.2
3.4.2	**Credit ratings** Borrowers (and issuers of shares) are rated by outside agencies for their credit-worthiness. The lower their credit-rating, the higher the risk they will default. The higher the risk of default, the higher the interest rate (or dividend) they will have to offer.	4.5
3.4.3	**Personal credit ratings** Individuals build up a credit history, based on past borrowing and repayment patterns. People with poor credit histories have to pay much higher interest rates than people with good credit scores	4.6
3.4.4	**Secured vs unsecured lending** A loan secured on an asset, such as a house or flat, is less risky than an unsecured loan like an outstanding credit card balance. The interest rate will therefore usually be lower	4.7

ELEMENT 4	PROTECTION FROM RISKS	Chapter 4
	Individuals and other investors can take steps to protect themselves from risk	
4.1	**Insurance and insurance companies** Insurance is a way of transferring risk from individuals and firms to others – usually insurance companies	**1.1**
4.1.1	**Insurance premiums** Individuals pay fees called insurance premiums in return for a guarantee that they will be compensated for a specific loss – such as the theft of their car	1.2

Syllabus Unit/ Element		Chapter/ Section
4.1.2	**Insurance funds** Insurers collect these premiums together in a pool of money and use it to pay out compensation for insured losses. They try to ensure that the fund is always sufficient to cover any losses.	1.3
4.1.3	**Relationship between insurance premiums and risk** The higher the risk of a loss occurring, the higher the premium the insurance company will wish to charge	1.4
4.2	**Diversification** Just as individuals and firms can spread their risk with the help of an insurance company, investors can spread their risk by investing across many different types of investment or different geographical markets	**2**
4.2.1	**Diversification across different types of investment** Financial service providers can help investors identify a range of suitable investments, such as shares, bonds, property or commodities like gold. These are known as asset classes	2.1
4.2.2	**Geographical diversification** The economies of countries around the world experience different rates of growth: financial advisers can help investors spread their investments across different geographic markets to reduce the risk of being overly exposed to one particular market	2.2
4.2.3	**Portfolio investment** With the help of professional advice, investors build up a portfolio of investments with an overall risk profile with which they feel comfortable	2.3
4.3	**Collective investment** Small investors with insufficient money to spread across many different investments can 'pool' their money with other investors' money in collective investment schemes	**3**
4.3.1	**Diversification through collective investments** Collective investment schemes such as unit trusts enable investors to spread small sums of money across a range of financial assets in a range of different markets. The benefits of this level of diversification would not otherwise be available to them	3.1
4.3.2	**Purchasing economies of scale** Buying in bulk is usually cheaper than buying in small amounts. Collective investment schemes enable small investors to take advantage of these 'purchasing economies of scale'	3.2
4.3.3	**Management economies of scale** By clubbing together in a collective investment scheme, small investors can afford to pay for expert financial advice	3.3
4.4	**Syndication** Risk can be spread through syndication	**4**

Syllabus Unit/ Element		Chapter/ Section
4.4.1	**Loan syndication** Banks and other lenders can spread their risk on very large loans by setting up a syndicate and parcelling up the loan among the syndicate members	4
4.4.2	**Insurance syndication and reinsurance** Insurers can spread their risk by insuring jointly with other insurance companies working as a syndicate, or they can insure themselves with other insurance companies (this is known as reinsurance).	4.2
ELEMENT 5	**COMPETING FOR OUR MONEY**	**Chapter 5**
	Banks and building societies compete with each other to attract savers' deposits. Companies compete to attract investors' money – either in the form of shares (equities) or loans (bonds)	**1**
5.1	**Calculating the return on an investment** Investors choose where to invest their money on the basis of projected total return over the life of the investment. Total return is the combination of income and capital gain arising from that investment	**2**
5.1.1	**Yield** Yield is the income from an investment expressed as a percentage of the initial outlay for that investment. Examples: interest as a percentage of a savings deposit or dividend as a percentage of a share's purchase price, or interest as a percentage of a bond's purchase price	2.1
5.1.2	**Capital gain (or loss)** The difference between the purchase price of an investment (such as a property, share or bond) and its current market price is called a capital gain (or loss, as the case may be). It is usually expressed as a percentage of the original purchase price. This gain (or loss) is only realised if the investment is actually sold	2
5.1.3	**Total return** To calculate total return, divide the selling price of the investment plus any dividends/interest received, by its total cost	2
5.2	**Yields** If the intention is to hold onto an investment for the income and not to realise any capital gain by selling it, the yield alone must compare favourably with those of other competing investments	**2.4**
5.2.1	**Required yield** Investors will require a higher yield in return for taking on a higher risk. Investors in shares, for instance, will require a higher yield than they would on cash deposits at a bank	2.3
5.2.2	**Yield advantage** Yield advantage is the extent by which the yield on one investment exceeds the yield on another investment with a similar risk profile	2.2

Syllabus Unit/ Element		Chapter/ Section
5.2.3	**Competing on yield** If a rival investment starts offering a higher yield, to stay competitive, other investments must either increase their yield too. If they do not, investors will switch to the higher-yielding investment	2.2
5.3	**Price/yield correlation** If the income stream (eg, interest or dividend) from an investment cannot be increased, the only way to increase the yield is for the price to fall (because yield = income/price x 100). When price goes down, yield goes up, and vice versa	**2.2**
5.3.1	**Positive correlation: interest rates and rent** If interest rates rise, investors in buy-to-let flats will demand higher rents to restore the yield advantage of their investment	3.3
5.3.2	**Negative correlation: interest rates and bond prices** If interest rates rise, bond prices will fall because bonds pay a fixed rate of interest	2.3

ELEMENT 6	THE ROLE OF GOVERNMENTS IN AN ECONOMY	Chapter 6
	Central banks act on behalf of their governments in setting interest rates for an economy. Governments also intervene in the economy directly through the setting of taxes, the spending of tax revenue on public services and by the creation of laws that govern the way people do business	1
6.1	**Monetary policy** Central banks, such as the Bank of England, set the rate of interest at which they will lend to the banking system. These form the 'base' rate from which all other interest rates are derived	**1.1**
6.1.1	**Use of interest rates to control consumer spending** With so much consumer spending relying on borrowed money, the more expensive money is to borrow, the less spending there will be in an economy – and vice versa	1.1.1
6.1.2	**Saving and interest rates** Higher interest rates make savings accounts more attractive as an investment, which makes other investments such as equities and bonds appear less attractive	1.2
6.2	**Fiscal policy** Governments impose taxes on income and spending to fund spending on public services such as health and education. Governments also borrow money from investors when tax revenue is insufficient to cover their planned expenditure	**2**
6.2.1	**Taxation** Governments impose taxes directly, through income and corporation tax; and indirectly through VAT	2.1

Syllabus Unit/ Element		Chapter/ Section
6.2.2	**"Leaning against the wind"** Governments will often spend more when the economy is growing too slowly and cut back on spending when the economy is growing too fast	2.2
6.3	**Borrowing** Governments borrow mainly through the issuance of bonds. In the UK, government bonds are called 'gilts' and account for a large proportion of the bond market	**3**
6.3.1	**Fiscal deficits** When governments try to counteract the effects of economic recession, they often spend more than their revenue	3.1
6.3.2	**Government debt** Fiscal deficits can build up year after year, until countries are so overwhelmed by debt that investors are unwilling to lend them any more	3.2
6.4	**Role of the financial regulators** Economies require a stable and well functioning financial system. Governments appoint regulators to ensure that banks and other financial service providers follow laws and treat their customers fairly	**4**
6.4.1	**The Bank of England** The Bank of England sets interest rates through its Monetary Policy Committee; it regulates banks and other financial firms through the Prudential Regulation Authority	4.1
6.4.2	**Financial Conduct Authority** The Financial Conduct Authority regulates the way financial services firms deal with their customers and with each other	4.2

ELEMENT 7	THE ROLE OF GOVERNMENTS IN AN ECONOMY	Chapter 7
	In Europe, governments account for about 40-60% of economic activity, depending on the individual country. The remainder is undertaken by the private sector, operating in markets where the interaction between households and firms establishes the supply and demand for goods and services	1
7.1	**Households and firms** Economists divide up the private sector into households and firms. The two interact in a circular flow of buying and selling of goods and services	**1.1**
7.1.1	**Households** Individuals are grouped together in households. Households wish to buy goods and services provided by firms – but only at a price they are willing to pay: this is called 'demand'	1.1.1

Syllabus Unit/ Element		Chapter/ Section
7.1.2	**Firms** Firms wish to sell goods and services to the households. The willingness to sell a good or service at a given price is called 'supply'	1.1.2
7.2	**Factors of production** There are four key inputs that go into the making of any good or the supply of any service: land, labour, capital and enterprise	**2**
7.2.1	**Land** The term 'land' is used to cover all the physical resources needed, such as: fields required for agriculture; the factory used for manufacturing; the shop used for a retail business; the office used by a service company	2.1
7.2.2	**Labour** 'Labour' is the workforce: skilled, unskilled or a mix of both. Labour is supplied by households	2.2
7.2.3	**Capital** 'Capital' is the plant and equipment used to produce goods or services. Examples of capital goods range from welding robots on a car production line to ATM machines used by banks to dispense cash to their customers	2.3
7.2.4	**Enterprise** 'Enterprise' is sometimes also known as 'entrepreneurship'. It is the know-how or ability to combine the three other factors in order to make a good or provide a service.	2.4
7.3	**Factor incomes** Each factor of production earns income in a different way	**3**
7.3.1	**Land earns rent** Land earns rent	3.1
7.3.2	**Labour earns wages** Wages are the main way in which households earn the money they need to buy goods or services from the firms	3.2
7.3.3	**Capital earns interest** The money used to buy capital goods is also known as capital and is usually provided by investors or lenders. Investors and lenders seek a return on their money and they receive this in the form of dividends or interest	3.3
7.3.4	**Enterprise earns profits** Entrepreneurs seek a reward for their expertise, know-how and energy in the form of profits. If they cannot earn profits, they will take their talents elsewhere	3.4
7.4	**Profit maximisation** Firms are presumed always to be trying to maximise their profits by buying at the lowest price and selling at the highest	**4**

Syllabus Unit/ Element		Chapter/ Section
7.4.1	**Potential for conflict** The desire of firms to maximise their profits can lead them into conflict with workers, who wish to maximise their wages, and with governments, who seek the greatest output at the lowest possible cost	4.2

ELEMENT 8	THE FUNCTIONS OF MARKETS	Chapter 8
	Wants are unlimited but the resources to satisfy those wants are scarce. Markets are the means by which economies find a balance between those two	**1**
8.1	**The price mechanism** In any properly functioning market, price will establish equilibrium between the supply of goods and services and the demand for those goods and services	**1.1**
8.1.1	**Market clearing price** The market clearing price is the price at which suppliers are willing to sell all their goods or services and customers are willing to buy	1.1.1
8.1.2	**High price as a signal** A high price signals to producers that demand is greater than supply: they will produce more to take advantage of that high demand	1.1.2
8.1.3	**Low price as a signal** A low price signals to producers that supply is greater than demand: they will cut back production	1.1.2
8.2	**Examples of markets in action** Markets set the price for almost every type of human activity or need	**2**
8.2.1	**Commodity markets** Commodity markets set the price of essentials such as wheat, copper or electricity	2.1
8.2.2	**Labour markets** Households will withdraw their labour if the wages on offer are too low and alternative, higher-paying jobs are available. During periods of high unemployment, workers' bargaining power is limited	3.1
8.3	**Financial markets** Financial markets play a key part in the pricing of interest rates for savings, loans and foreign exchange rates	**2.3**
8.3.1	**Money markets** Banks and other financial institutions lend money to each other. The interest rate they charge is often used as a benchmark, on which the interest charged on many other financial products is based	2.4

Syllabus Unit/ Element		Chapter/ Section
8.3.2	**Stock exchanges** Stock exchanges are markets where shares (equities) and loans (bonds) are traded. Stock exchanges match buyers and sellers automatically based on price	2.4.1
8.3.3	**Foreign exchange markets** Foreign exchange transactions amount to more than US$1trn a day, but do not take place on formal exchanges. Buyers and sellers contact each other directly	2.4.2
8.4	**When markets do not work properly** Sometimes markets do not function well or fail to function at all	**3**
8.4.1	**Missing markets** Markets cannot exist where there is no practical way to charge people for using a good or service. Examples are radio programmes or street lights.	3.2
8.4.2	**Market failure** Sometimes markets do not allocate resources in the most efficient way. Governments will often then intervene to correct the market failure	3.3
8.4.3	**Information failure** Sometimes people do not act in their own best interests because they lack sufficient information to make an informed decision. Young people rarely save enough for their retirement because they do not understand the cost of living for old people and the limitations of the basic state pension	3.4

ELEMENT 9	PLANNING FOR THE FUTURE	Chapter 9
	Many people wish to buy their own home at some point in their lives, and everyone has to retire. These require substantial sums to be saved. The earlier people start to save, the better	1
9.1	**Savings and investments** Financial service providers offer a number of products to help people save. These include life assurance products, individual savings accounts (ISAs)	2
9.1.1	**Individual Savings Accounts (ISAs) and Junior ISAs; Stocks and shares ISAs** ISAs and Junior ISAs are tax-exempt ways of saving cash; a stocks and shares ISA lets you put money into different types of investments, such as collective investment scheme. This means your investment can go down as well as up.	2.1
9.1.2	**Government-guaranteed savings products** National Savings & Investments (NS&I): Premium Bonds and savings accounts	2.2

Syllabus Unit/ Element		Chapter/ Section
9.1.3	**Life assurance** As well as protecting themselves against accidental death, savers can take out life assurance policies that pay out guaranteed sums on retirement	2.3
9.2	**Pensions** Pensions provide a regular income for people after retirement	**3**
9.2.1	**Basic State Pension** Provided they have built up sufficient National Insurance Contributions over their working lives, retirees are paid a weekly pension by the state. It covers around half of the estimated living costs for a retired person, so additional pension provision is considered essential	3.1
9.2.2	**National Employment Savings Trust (NEST)** All employees in the UK are now enrolled automatically in a workplace pension scheme. The aim is to help people make up for the shortcomings of the basic State Pension	3.2
9.2.3	**Other pension schemes** Employers may offer other, so-called 'occupational' pensions schemes for their employees. Some of these require the employee to contribute part of their wages or salary to the pension scheme. Individuals can also set up their own personal pension schemes	3.3
9.3	**Annuities** Most pension schemes aim to build up a pension 'pot', which upon retired is sold to a financial services provider in return for a sum of money paid annually. This payment is called an annuity	**4**
9.3.1	**Annuities and life expectancy** The longer the provider expects the annuity buyer to live, the lower will be the annual payment offered and vice versa. That is why smokers and other people with impaired life expectancy can expect higher annuity rates	4.1

ELEMENT 10	STEWARDSHIP: THE ETHICS OF BUSINESS	Chapter 10
	Stewardship is the concept of looking after someone's property as if it were one's own	**1**
10.1	**Looking after someone's savings** When people entrust their life savings to others, they have a right to expect the highest levels of due care and attention. That is why financial service providers have a duty of stewardship	**1.1**

Syllabus Unit/ Element		Chapter/ Section
10.1.1	**Customers** The customers of financial services providers have a right to be treated fairly. The UK's financial regulation system is focused on this aim	1.2
10.1.2	**Treating customers fairly** The customers of financial services providers have a right to be treated fairly. The UK's financial regulation system is focused on this aim	1.2
10.2	**Looking after someone's company** Directors of companies are entrusted by the shareholders to run the company in a prudent but profitable way; but many others have a stake in the way in which a company is run	**2**
10.2.1	**Stakeholders** Stakeholders in a company include shareholders, employees, customers, and the government. They all rely on the directors and managers to run the company well	2.1
10.2.2	**Pay and bonuses** The directors and managers of companies should not enrich themselves at the expense of their stakeholders	2.1
10.3	**Looking after the tax-payers' money** **The government has responsibility to its citizens to use state funds wisely and fairly**	**3**
10.3.1	**State-owned banks** As a consequence of the financial crisis of 2007-08, several banks are now owned by the government. The government has a duty to ensure that these banks provide a return for the tax-payer, while also performing their commercial function of taking deposits and lending to firms and individuals	3

Assessment Objectives and Weightings

Each examination paper is constructed from a specification that determines the weightings that will be given to each element. The specification is given below.

It is important to note that the numbers quoted may vary slightly from examination to examination as there is some flexibility to ensure that each examination has a consistent level of difficulty. .

Element Number	Element	Questions
1	Buying and Selling	4
2	The Value of Money Now and in the Future	4
3	Risk and Reward	3
4	Protection from Risks	3
5	Competing for Our Money	2
6	The Role of Governments in an Economy	3
7	The Role of the Private Sector in an Economy	2
8	The Functions of Markets	3
9	Planning for the Future	3
10	Stewardship: The Ethics of Business	3
Total		**30**

CISI Associate (ACSI) Membership can work for you...

Studying for a CISI qualification is hard work and we're sure you're putting in plenty of hours, but don't lose sight of your goal!

This is just the first step in your career; there is much more to achieve!

The securities and investments industry attracts ambitious and driven individuals. You're probably one yourself and that's great, but on the other hand you're almost certainly surrounded by lots of other people with similar ambitions.

So how can you stay one step ahead during these uncertain times?

Entry Criteria:
Pass in either:
- Investment Operations Certificate (IOC), IFQ, ICWM, Capital Markets in, eg, Securities, Derivatives or Investment Management, Advanced Certificates; or
- one CISI Diploma/Masters in Wealth Management paper

Joining Fee: £25 or free if applying via prefilled application form   **Annual Subscription (pro rata):** £125

Using your new CISI qualification* to become an Associate (ACSI) member of the Chartered Institute for Securities & Investment could well be the next important career move you make this year, and help you maintain your competence.

Join our global network of over 40,000 financial services professionals and start enjoying both the professional and personal benefits that CISI membership offers. Once you become a member you can use the prestigious ACSI designation after your name and even work towards becoming personally chartered.

* ie, Investment Operations Certificate (IOC), IFQ, ICWM, Capital Markets

Benefits in Summary...
- Use of the CISI CPD Scheme
- Unlimited free CPD seminars, webcasts, podcasts and online training tools
- Highly recognised designatory letters
- Unlimited free attendance at CISI Professional Forums
- CISI publications including *S&I Review* and *Change – The Regulatory Update*
- 20% discount on all CISI conferences and training courses
- Invitation to CISI Annual Lecture
- Select Benefits – our exclusive personal benefits portfolio

The ACSI designation will provide you with access to a range of member benefits, including Professional Refresher where there are currently over 50 modules available on subjects including Behavioural Finance, Cybercrime and Conduct Risk. CISI TV is also available to members, allowing you to catch up on the latest CISI events, whilst earning valuable CPD hours.

Plus many other networking opportunities which could be invaluable for your career.

Revision Express Interactive

You've bought the workbook... now test your knowledge before your exam.

Revision Express Interactive is an engaging online study tool to be used in conjunction with CISI workbooks. It contains exercises and revision questions.

Key Features of Revision Express Interactive:
- Examination-focused – the content of Revision Express Interactive covers the key points of the syllabus
- Questions throughout to reaffirm understanding of the subject
- Special end-of-module practice exam to reflect as closely as possible the standard you will experience in your exam (please note, however, they are not the CISI exam questions themselves)
- Interactive exercises throughout
- Extensive glossary of terms
- Useful associated website links
- Allows you to study whenever you like

IMPORTANT: The questions contained in Revision Express Interactive elearning products are designed as aids to revision, and should not be seen in any way as mock exams.

Price per elearning module: £35
Price when purchased with the CISI workbook: £100 (normal price: £110)

To purchase Revision Express Interactive:

call our Customer Support Centre on:
+44 20 7645 0777

or visit CISI Online Bookshop at:
cisi.org/bookshop

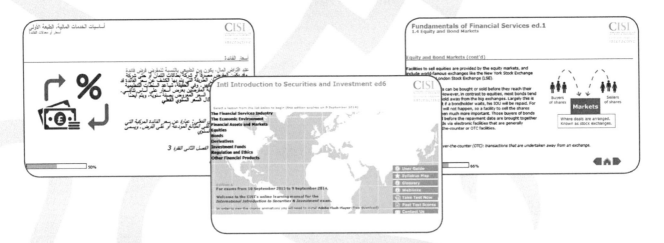

For more information on our elearning products, contact our Customer Support Centre on +44 20 7645 0777, or visit our website at cisi.org/study

Professional Refresher

Self-testing elearning modules to refresh your knowledge, meet regulatory and firm requirements, and earn CPD hours.

Professional Refresher is a training solution to help you remain up-to-date with industry developments, maintain regulatory compliance and demonstrate continuing learning.

This popular online learning tool allows self-administered refresher testing on a variety of topics, including the latest regulatory changes.

There are currently over 50 modules available which address UK and international issues. Modules are reviewed by practitioners frequently and new topics are added to the suite on a regular basis.

Benefits to firms:
- Learning and tests can form part of business T&C programme
- Learning and tests kept up to date and accurate by the CISI
- Relevant and useful – devised by industry practitioners
- Access to individual results available as part of management overview facility, 'Super User'
- Records of staff training can be produced for internal use and external audits
- Cost-effective – no additional charge for CISI members
- Available to non-members

Benefits to individuals:
- Comprehensive selection of topics across industry sectors
- Modules are frequently reviewed and updated by industry experts
- New topics introduced regularly
- Free for members
- Successfully passed modules are recorded in your CPD log as Active Learning
- Counts as structured learning for RDR purposes
- On completion of a module, a certificate can be printed out for your own records

The full suite of Professional Refresher modules is free to CISI members or £150 for non-members. Modules are also available individually. To view a full list of Professional Refresher modules visit:

cisi.org/refresher

If you or your firm would like to find out more contact our Client Relationship Management team:
+ 44 20 7645 0670
crm@cisi.org

For more information on our elearning products, contact our Customer Support Centre on +44 20 7645 0777, or visit our website at cisi.org/study

Professional Refresher

Top 5

Integrity & Ethics
- High Level View
- Ethical Behaviour
- An Ethical Approach
- Compliance vs Ethics

Anti-Money Laundering
- Introduction to Money Laundering
- UK Legislation and Regulation
- Money Laundering Regulations 2007
- Proceeds of Crime Act 2002
- Terrorist Financing
- Suspicious Activity Reporting
- Money Laundering Reporting Officer
- Sanctions

Financial Crime
- What is Financial Crime?
- Insider Dealing and Market Abuse Introduction, Legislation, Offences and Rules
- Money Laundering Legislation, Regulations, Financial Sanctions and Reporting Requirements
- Money Laundering and the Role of the MLRO

Information Security and Data Protection
- Information Security: The Key Issues
- Latest Cybercrime Developments
- The Lessons From High-Profile Cases
- Key Identity Issues: Know Your Customer
- Implementing the Data Protection Act 1998
- The Next Decade: Predictions For The Future

UK Bribery Act
- Background to the Act
- The Offences
- What the Offences Cover
- When Has an Offence Been Committed
- The Defences Against Charges of Bribery
- The Penalties

Compliance

Behavioural Finance
- Background to Behavioural Finance
- Biases and Heuristics
- The Regulator's Perspective
- Implications of Behavioural Finance

Conduct Risk
- What is Conduct Risk?
- Regulatory Powers
- Managing Conduct Risk
- Treating Customers Fairly
- Practical Application of Conduct Risk

Conflicts of Interest
- Introduction
- Examples of Conflicts of Interest
- Examples of Enforcement Action
- Policies and Procedures
- Tools to Manage Conflicts of Interest
- Conflict Management Process
- Good Practice

Risk (an overview)
- Definition of Risk
- Key Risk Categories
- Risk Management Process
- Risk Appetite
- Business Continuity
- Fraud and Theft
- Information Security

T&C Supervision Essentials
- Who Expects What From Supervisors?
- Techniques for Effective Routine Supervision
- Practical Skills of Guiding and Coaching
- Developing and Assessing New Advisers
- Techniques for Resolving Poor Performance

Operations

Best Execution
- What Is Best Execution?
- Achieving Best Execution
- Order Execution Policies
- Information to Clients & Client Consent
- Monitoring, the Rules, and Instructions
- Client Order Handling

Central Clearing
- Background to Central Clearing
- The Risks CCPs Mitigate
- The Events of 2007/08
- Target 2 Securities

Corporate Actions
- Corporate Structure and Finance
- Life Cycle of an Event
- Mandatory Events
- Voluntary Events

Wealth

Client Assets and Client Money
- Protecting Client Assets and Client Money
- Ring-Fencing Client Assets and Client Money
- Due Diligence of Custodians
- Reconciliations
- Records and Accounts
- CASS Oversight

Investment Principles and Risk
- Diversification
- Factfind and Risk Profiling
- Investment Management
- Modern Portfolio Theory and Investing Styles
- Direct and Indirect Investments
- Socially Responsible Investment
- Collective Investments
- Investment Trusts
- Dealing in Debt Securities and Equities

Principles of RDR
- Professionalism – Qualifications
- Professionalism – SPS
- Description of Advice – Part 1
- Description of Advice – Part 2
- Adviser Charging

Suitability of Client Investments
- Assessing Suitability
- Risk Profiling and Establishing Risk
- Obtaining Customer Information
- Suitable Questions and Answers
- Making Suitable Investment Selections
- Guidance, Reports and Record Keeping

International

Dodd-Frank Act
- Background and Purpose
- Creation of New Regulatory Bodies
- Too Big to Fail and the Volcker Rule
- Regulation of Derivatives
- Securitisation
- Credit Rating Agencies

Foreign Account Tax Compliance Act (FATCA)
- Reporting by US Taxpayers
- Reporting by Foreign Financial Institutions
- Implementation Timeline

Sovereign Wealth Funds
- Definition and History
- The Major SWFs
- Transparency Issues
- The Future
- Sources

cisi.org/refresher

Feedback to the CISI

Have you found this workbook to be a valuable aid to your studies? We would like your views, so please email us at learningresources@cisi.org with any thoughts, ideas or comments.

Accredited Training Providers

Support for examination students studying for the Chartered Institute for Securities & Investment (CISI) Qualifications is provided by several Accredited Training Providers (ATPs), including Fitch Learning and BPP. The CISI's ATPs offer a range of face-to-face training courses, distance learning programmes, their own learning resources and study packs which have been accredited by the CISI. The CISI works in close collaboration with its ATPs to ensure they are kept informed of changes to CISI examinations so they can build them into their own courses and study packs.

CISI Workbook Specialists Wanted

Workbook Authors

Experienced freelance authors with finance experience, and who have published work in their area of specialism, are sought. Responsibilities include:

- Updating workbooks in line with new syllabuses and any industry developments
- Ensuring that the syllabus is fully covered

Workbook Reviewers

Individuals with a high-level knowledge of the subject area are sought. Responsibilities include:

- Highlighting any inconsistencies against the syllabus
- Assessing the author's interpretation of the workbook

Workbook Technical Reviewers

Technical reviewers provide a detailed review of the workbook and bring the review comments to the panel. Responsibilities include:

- Cross-checking the workbook against the syllabus
- Ensuring sufficient coverage of each learning objective

Workbook Proofreaders

Proofreaders are needed to proof workbooks both grammatically and also in terms of the format and layout. Responsibilities include:

- Checking for spelling and grammar mistakes
- Checking for formatting inconsistencies

If you are interested in becoming a CISI external specialist call:
+44 20 7645 0609

or email:
iain.worman@cisi.org

For bookings, orders, membership and general enquiries please contact our Customer Support Centre on +44 20 7645 0777, or visit our website at cisi.org